Richard Baxter

RICHARD BAXTER

Christian Focus

ISBN 1 85792 380 4
© Christian Focus Publications

This edition published in 1998 by Christian Focus Publications,
Geanies House, Fearn, Ross-shire, IV20 1TW, Great Britain.
Cover design by Donna Macleod

Previously published by the Religious Tract Society, this new
edition has been slightly edited. The reader should bear in
mind, however, that editorial comments in the text reflect the
situation in Great Britain during the nineteenth century and
not necessarily the situation today.

Contents

1

Early Life and Conversion

Richard Baxter was born at Rowton, Shropshire, on the 12th of November, 1615. He resided in that village with his maternal grandfather till he was nearly ten years of age, when he was taken home to live with his parents at Eaton Constantine, in the same county.

His father, he says, 'had the competent estate of a freeholder, free from the temptations of poverty and riches; but, having been addicted to gaming in his youth, and his father before him, it was so entangled by debts, that it occasioned some excess of worldly cares before it was freed.'

About the time of his son's birth, he became seriously impressed with the importance of Divine truth, and appears to have subsequently become a sincere follower of the Redeemer. His conversion was effected chiefly through the instrumentality of reading the Scriptures. He had but few opportunities of attending on the ordinary means of grace. Many of the pulpits were occupied by ministers ignorant of the truth as it is in Jesus; and those who preached the gospel in its purity were, for the most part, so despised and contemned, that it required no small share of moral courage to attend on their ministry. Converted himself, he became anxious for the salvation of his only son. He directed the attention of his youthful charge to the sacred Scriptures, whence he had himself derived so much benefit. Nor were his instructions and efforts altogether vain. Baxter thus ingenuously confesses his early sins and convictions, in his history of his own life and times:

'At first my father set me to read the historical parts of the Scripture, which, suiting with my nature, greatly delighted me; and though all that time I neither understood nor relished much the doctrinal part, and mystery of redemption, yet it did me good by acquainting me with the matters of fact, and drawing me on to love the Bible, and to search by degrees into the rest.

'But though my conscience would trouble me when I sinned, yet divers sins I was addicted to, and often committed against my conscience; which, for the warning of others, I will here confess to my shame.

'1. I was much addicted, when I feared correction, to lie, that I might escape.

'2. I was much addicted to the excessive gluttonous eating of apples and pears, which, I think laid the foundation of that weakness of my stomach, which caused the bodily calamities of my life.

'3. To this end, and to concur with naughty boys that gloried in evil, I have often gone into other men's orchards, and stolen their fruit, when I had enough at home.

'4. I was somewhat excessively addicted to play and that with covetousness, for money.

'5. I was extremely bewitched with a love of romances, fables, and old tales, which corrupted my affections, and lost my time.

'6. I was guilty of much idle foolish chat, and imitation of boys in scurrilous foolish words and actions, though I durst not swear.

'7. I was too proud of my masters' commendations for learning, who all of them fed my pride, making me seven or eight years the highest in the school, and boasting of me to others; which, though it furthered my learning, yet helped not my humility.

'8. I was too bold and irreverent towards my parents.

'These were my sins, which, in my childhood, conscience troubled me for a great while before they were overcome.'

His convictions gathered strength, although occasionally resisted. The temptations to neglect religion were strong and powerful. The reproach cast on his father and others, who, for their desire and pursuit of holiness, were contemptuously designated 'Puritans', proved for a season a stumbling-block in his path. Still, however, the reflecting mind of the son led him to discern the difference between the conduct of his father and that of his calumniators, and to conclude that there was more of reason and truth in a life of holiness than in a life of impiety and rebellion against the Majesty of heaven. He says:

'In the village where I lived, the reader read the common prayer briefly; and the rest of the day, even till dark night almost, except eating time, was spent in dancing under a maypole and a great tree, not far from my father's door, where all the town did meet together: and though one of my father's own tenants was the piper, he could not restrain him, nor break the sport; so that we could not read the Scripture in our family without the great disturbance of the tabor and pipe, and noise in the street![1]

'Many times my mind was inclined to be among them, and sometimes I broke loose from conscience, and joined with them; and the more I did it the more I was inclined to

---

1. These profanations of the Lord's day were authorized and encouraged by the royal proclamation, called the Book of Sports, set forth in 1618.

it. But when I heard them call my father "Puritan", it did much to cure me and alienate me from them; for I considered that my father's exercise of reading the Scripture was better than theirs, and would surely be better thought on by all men at the last; and I considered what it was for that he and others were thus derided. When I heard them speak scornfully of others, as puritans, whom I never knew, I was at first apt to believe all the lies and slanders wherewith they loaded them; but when I heard my own father so reproached, and perceived the drunkards were the forwardest in the reproach, I perceived that it was mere malice.

'For my father never scrupled common prayer or ceremonies, nor spoke against bishops, nor ever so much as prayed but by a book or form, being not acquainted then with any that did otherwise. But only for reading Scripture when the rest were dancing on the Lord's day, and for praying, but a form out of the end of the common prayer-book, in his house, and for reproving drunkards and swearers, and for talking sometimes a few words of Scripture, and about the life to come, he was reviled commonly by the name of Puritan, Precisian, and Hypocrite; and so were the godly conformable ministers that lived anywhere in the country near us, not only by our neighbours, but by the common talk of the vulgar rabble of all about us. By his experience I was fully convinced that godly people were the best; and those that despised them, and lived in sin and pleasure, were a malignant, unhappy sort of people; and this kept me out of their company, except now and then, when the love of sports and play enticed me.'

When about fifteen years of age, 'it pleased God,' he writes, 'of his wonderful mercy, to open my eyes with a clearer insight into the concerns and case of my own soul, and to touch my heart with a livelier feeling of things spiritual than ever I had found before.' While under this concern, a poor man in the town lent his father an old torn book, entitled *Bunny's Resolutions*. 'In reading this book,' he observes, 'it pleased God to awaken my soul, and show me the folly of sinning, and the misery of the wicked, and the inexpressible weight of things eternal, and the necessity of resolving on a holy life, more than I was ever acquainted with before. The same things which I knew before came now in another manner, with light, and sense, and seriousness to my heart.

'Yet whether sincere conversion began now, or before, or after, I was never able to this day to know; for I had before had some love to the things and people which were good, and a restraint from other sins, except those forementioned; and so much from those that I seldom committed most of them, and when I did, it was with great reluctance. And, both now and formerly, I knew that Christ was the only Mediator, by whom we must have pardon, justification, and life: but even at that time I had little lively sense of the love of God in Christ to the world or me, nor of my special need of him!

'About this time it pleased God that a poor pedlar came to the door, that had ballads and some good books, and my father bought of him Dr. Sibbes' *Bruised Reed*. This also I read, and found it suited to my taste, and seasonably sent me; which opened more the love of God to me, and gave me a livelier apprehension of the mystery of redemption, and how much I was beholden to Jesus Christ.

'After this, we had a servant that had a little piece of Mr. Perkins's works, *Of Repentance*, and the *Right Art of*

Living and Dying Well, and the *Government of the Tongue*; and the reading of these did further inform me, and confirm me. And thus, without any means but books, was God pleased to resolve me for himself.'

Various are the means by which God awakens the soul to a sense of its danger, and lead it to the knowledge and enjoyment of himself. The pulpit and the school, conversation and reading, correspondence and advice, have been employed as instruments in the hands of the Eternal Spirit in effecting the conversion of souls. To preaching, as the express appointment of God, must be ascribed the highest place; but inferior only to it is the instrumentality of reading religious books especially. In places where the preaching of the gospel is unknown or unattended, the distribution of religious books is of the utmost importance. To such books Baxter was greatly indebted for his conversion: and having derived so much benefit from this means, he ever after employed it extensively among his friends, his flock, and all to whom his influence would reach.[2] In the formation of Baxter's early religious opinions and character, we see the instrumentality of a labourer, a pedlar, and a servant employed. The sovereignty of God is

2. The facilities afforded in the present day for the dissemination of religious knowledge are truly astonishing; and, among others, the efforts of the Religious Tract Society, with its millions of publications, should not be overlooked. Many will arise in the last day, and acknowledge that their conversion was effected by means of its publications. Nor is it the least advantage of this and similar institutions, that they afford an opportunity to persons in the humblest circumstances to be instrumental in doing good to their fellow-creatures. They can give a tract, though they cannot deliver a discourse; they can send a tract where they cannot visit in person; they can circulate books where they cannot engage in religious conversations.

clearly seen in the agents and means of salvation. 'His wisdom is unsearchable, and his ways are past finding out.' 'To God only wise be all the glory.'

Baxter's early education was greatly neglected. His professed teachers were either incompetent to their task, or suffered him to be occupied rather as he chose than according to any regular rule. Notwithstanding this neglect and irregularity, he made considerable progress. He rose superior to every difficulty, and in due time became qualified to enter the university. He was persuaded, however, not to enter college, but to pursue his studies under the direction of Mr Wickstead, chaplain to the council, at Ludlow Castle. Being his only pupil, it was expected that, through the undivided attention of his tutor, his proficiency would be greater than either at Cambridge or Oxford. The preceptor became much attached to the pupil; but, being in earnest quest of place and preferment, he neglected his charge. He allowed him 'books and time enough', but never seriously attempted to instruct his mind.

Nor was this the only disadvantage attending his residence at Ludlow; for he was thrown into gay and fashionable society, and was exposed to the various temptations incident to such a situation. His religious principles were in danger of being corrupted or destroyed by the practice of gambling; but he was enabled, by the grace of God, to escape the snare, and to resist all subsequent attempts to lead him astray. In this situation he formed an intimacy with a young man of professed seriousness and piety, but who at length, by the seductive influence of liquor, became an apostate. At this period, however, he instructed young Baxter 'in the way of God more perfectly', prayed with him, exhorted and encouraged him in his religious course, and thus became of essential service to his young friend.

Baxter remained with his tutor about a year and a half, and then returned home. At the request of Lord Newport, he took the charge of the grammar school at Wroxeter for a short time, as the master was in a dying state. On his death, Baxter left his charge, and pursued his studies and religious inquiries under the direction of the venerable Mr Garbett, a minister of Wroxeter.

The health of Baxter was in a precarious state, and, in the prospect of eternity, he became more solicitous to improve his remaining days in the worship, and ways, and service of God. He says:

'Being in expectation of death, by a violent cough, with spitting of blood, etc., of two years' continuance, supposed to be a deep degree of a consumption, I was yet more awakened to be serious and solicitous about my soul's everlasting state; and I came so short of that sense and seriousness, which a matter of such infinite weight required, that I was many years in doubt of my sincerity, and thought I had no spiritual life at all. I wondered at the senseless hardness of my heart, that I could think and talk of sin and hell, and Christ and grace, of God and heaven, with no more feeling. I cried out from day to day to God for grace against this senseless deadness. I called myself the most hard-hearted sinner, that could feel nothing of all that I knew and talked of. I was not then sensible of the incomparable excellence of holy love, and delight in God, nor much employed in thanksgiving and praise; but all my groans were for more contrition, and a broken heart, and I prayed most for tears and tenderness.

'And thus I complained for many years to God and man; and between the expectations of death, and the doubts of my own sincerity in grace, I was kept in some more care of my salvation, than my nature, too stupid and too far from melancholy, was easily brought to.

'Thus was I long kept with the calls of approaching death at one ear, and the questionings of a doubtful conscience at the other; and since then I have found that this method of God's was very wise, and no other was so likely to have tended to my good. These benefits of it I sensibly perceived as:

'1. It made me vile and loathsome to myself, and made pride one of the most hateful sins in the world to me. I thought of myself as I now think of a detestable sinner, and my enemy; that is, with a love of benevolence, wishing them well, but with little love of complacency at all: and the long continuance of it tended the more effectually to a habit.

'2. It much restrained me from that sportful levity and vanity which my nature and youthfulness did much incline me to, and caused me to meet temptations to sensuality with the greatest fear, and made them less effectual against me.

'3. It made the doctrine of redemption the more savoury to me, and my thoughts of Christ to be more serious and regardful, than before they were. I remember, in the beginning, how savoury to my reading was Mr. Perkin's short treatise of the *Right Knowledge of Christ Crucified*, and his *Exposition of the Creed*, because they taught me how to live by faith on Christ.

'4. It made the world seem to me as a carcase that had neither life nor loveliness, and it destroyed that ambitious desire after literary fame, which was the sin of my childhood. I had a desire before to have attained the highest academical degrees and reputation of learning, and to have chosen out my studies accordingly; but sickness, and solicitousness for my doubting soul, did shame away all these thoughts as fooleries and children's plays.

'5. It set me upon that method of my studies, which, since then, I have found the benefit of, though at the time I was not satisfied with myself. It caused me first to seek God's kingdom, and his righteousness, and most to mind the one thing needful; and to determine first of my ultimate end, by which I was engaged to choose out and prosecute all other studies as meant to that end. Therefore, divinity was not only carried on, with the rest of my studies, with an equal hand, but always had the first and chief place. And it caused me to study practical divinity first, in the most practical books, in a practical order; doing all purposely for the informing and reforming of my own soul.'

'And as for those doubts of my own salvation, which exercised me many years, the chief causes of them were these:

'1. Because I could not distinctly trace the workings of the Spirit upon my heart, in that method which Mr. Bolton, Mr. Hooker, Mr. Rogers, and other divines describe; nor knew the time of my conversion, being wrought on by the forementioned degrees. But, since then, I understood that the soul is in too dark and passionate a plight at first to be able to keep an exact account of the order of its own operations; and that preparatory grace being sometimes longer and sometimes shorter, and the first degree of special grace being usually very small, it is not possible that one of very many should be able to give any true account of the just time when special grace began, and advanced him above the state of preparation.

'2. My second doubt was as aforesaid, because of the hardness of my heart, or want of such lively apprehensions of things spiritual, which I had about things corporeal. And though I still groan under this as my sin and want, yet I now perceive that a soul in flesh doth work so much after the manner of the flesh, that it much desireth sensible apprehensions; but things spiritual and distant are not so apt to work upon them, and to stir the passions, as things present and sensible are.

'3. My next doubt was, lest education and fear had done all that ever was done upon my soul, and regeneration and love were yet to seek; because I had found convictions from my childhood, and found more fear than love in all my duties and restraints.

'But I afterward perceived that education is God's ordinary way for the conveyance of his grace, and ought no more to be set in opposition to the Spirit, than the preaching of the Word; and that it was the great mercy of God to begin with me so soon, and to prevent such sins as else might have been my shame and sorrow while I lived; and that repentance is good, but prevention and innocence better; which though we cannot attain in perfection, yet the more the better. And I understood, that, though fear without love be not a state of saving grace, and greater love to the world than to God be not consistent with sincerity, yet a little predominant love, prevailing against worldly love, conjoined with a far greater measure of fear, may be a state of special grace. And I found that my hearty love of the Word of God and of the servants of God, and my desires to be more holy, and especially the hatred of my heart for loving God no more, and my wish to love him, and be pleasing to him, was not without some love to himself, though it worked more sensibly on his nearer image.

'4. Another of my doubts was, because my grief and humiliation were no greater, and because I could weep no more for this.

'But I understood, at last, that God breaketh not all men's hearts alike, and that the gradual proceedings of his grace might be one cause, and my nature, not apt to weep for other things, another: and that the change of our heart from sin to God is true repentance, and a loathing of ourselves is true humiliation; and that he that had rather leave his sin than have leave to keep it, and had rather be the most holy than have leave to be unholy or less holy, is neither without true repentance nor the love of God.

'5. Another of my doubts was, because I had, after my change, committed some sins deliberately and knowingly. And, be they ever so small, I thought, he that could sin upon knowledge and deliberation had no true grace; and that, if I had but had as strong temptations to drunkenness, fraud, or other more heinous sins, I might also have committed them! And if these proved that I had then no saving grace, after all that I had felt, I thought it unlikely that ever I should have any.'

'The means by which God was pleased to give me some peace and comfort were:

'1. The reading of many consolatory books.

'2. The observation of other men's condition.

'When I heard many make the very same complaints that I did, who were people of whom I had the best esteem, for the uprightness and holiness of their lives, it much abated my fears and troubles. And, in particular, it much comforted me to read him whom I loved as one of the holiest of all the martyrs, John Bradford, subscribing himself so often, "The hard-hearted sinner," and "The miserable hard-hearted sinner," even as I was used to do myself.

3. 'And it much increased my peace when God's providence called me to the comforting of many others that had the same complaints. While I answered their doubts, I answered my own; and the charity which I was constrained to exercise for them redounded to myself, and insensibly abated my fears, and procured me an increase of quietness of mind.

'And yet, after all, I was glad of probabilities instead of full undoubted certainties; and to this very day, though I have no such degree of doubtfulness as is any great trouble to my soul, or procureth any great disquieting fears, yet I cannot say that I have such a certainty of my own sincerity in grace, as excludeth all doubts and fears of the contrary.'

Baxter's old preceptor induced him for a season to lay aside all thoughts respecting the ministry, and to become an attendant at court. He resided for a month at Whitehall, but became so disgusted with the scenes and practices of high life, that his conscience would not allow his longer continuance from home. He says: 'I had quickly enough of the court; when I saw a stage-play, instead of a sermon, on the Lord's Day in the afternoon, and saw what course was there in fashion, and heard little preaching but what was, as to one part, against the Puritans, I was glad to be gone. At the same time it pleased God that my mother fell sick and desired my return: and so I resolved to bid farewell to those kinds of employments and expectations.

'When I was going home again into the country, about Christmas Day, 1634, the greatest snow began that hath been in this age, which continued thence till Easter, at which some places had it many yards deep; and before it was a very hard frost, which necessitated me to frost-nail my horse twice or thrice a day. On the road I met a waggon loaded, where I had no passage by, but on the side of a bank, which, as I passed over, all my horse's feet slipped from under him, and all the girths brake, and so I was cast just before the waggon wheel, which had gone over me, but that it pleased God that suddenly the horses stopped, without any discernible cause, till I was recovered; which commanded me to observe the mercy of my Protector.'

On his return he found his mother extremely ill. She lingered till May, and then expired.

Baxter's own health was in a very precarious state; but he was anxiously desirous of doing good, during the short time which he supposed would be allotted to him on earth. He states:

'My own soul being under the serious apprehension of the matters of another world, I was exceedingly desirous to communicate those apprehensions to such ignorant, presumptuous, careless sinners, as the world aboundeth with. But I was in a very great perplexity between my encouragements and my discouragements. I was conscious of my personal insufficiency, for want of that measure of learning and experience, which so great and high a work required. I knew that the want of academical honours and degrees was likely to make me contemptible with the most, and consequently hinder the success of my endeavours. But yet, expecting to be so quickly in another world, the great concernments of miserable souls did prevail with me against all these impediments; and being conscious of a thirsty desire of men's conversion and salvation, and of some competent persuading faculty of expression, which fervent affections might help to actuate, I resolved, that if one or two souls only might be won to God, it would easily recompense all the dishonour which, for want of titles, I might undergo from men!'

2

Ordination and First Public Engagements

Baxter was induced, by the advice of his friend Berry, to accept the headmastership of a newly-endowed grammar school at Dudley, Worcestershire. He was the more ready to accept this situation, as it would afford him an opportunity of preaching in that unenlightened neighbourhood. He applied for ordination to the bishop of Winchester, which, after examination and subscription, was duly administered. He moreover received the bishop's licence to teach in the school at Dudley. In a subsequent period of his life, he dedicated his treatise on *Self-denial* to his friend, Colonel Berry, whose character had undergone a considerable change. The following passage from his dedicatory letter describes his views and feelings on entering the ministry, and his obligation to his friend and adviser.

'You brought me into the ministry. I am confident you know to what ends, and with what intentions I desired it. I was then very ignorant, young, and raw; though my weakness be yet such as I must lament, I must say, to the praise of the great Shepherd of the flock, that he hath, since then, offered me precious opportunities, much assistance, and as much encouragement as to any man that I know alive. You know my education and initial weakness were such as forbid me to glory in the flesh: but I will not rob God of his glory to avoid the appearance of ostentation, lest I be proud of seeming not to be proud. I doubt not but many thousand souls will thank you, when they have read that you were the man that led me into the ministry.

'Being settled in the new school at Dudley, I there preached my first public sermon in the upper parish church, and afterwards preached in the villages about, and there had occasion to fall afresh upon the study of conformity; for there were many private Christians thereabouts that were nonconformists, and one in the house with me. And that excellent man, Mr William Fenner, had lately lived two miles off, at Sedgeley, who, by defending conformity, and honouring it by a wonderfully powerful and successful way of preaching, conference, and holy living, had stirred up the nonconformists the more to a vehement pleading of their cause. And though they were there generally godly, honest people, yet smartly censorious, and made conformity no small fault. And they lent me manuscripts and books which I never saw before; whereupon I thought it my duty to set upon a serious, impartial trial of the whole cause.

'In the town of Dudley I lived, not a twelvemonth, in much comfort, amongst a poor, tractable people, lately noted for drunkenness, but commonly more ready to hear God's Word with submission and reformation, than most places where I have come; so that having, since the wars, set up a monthly lecture there, the church was usually as much crowded within, and at the windows, as ever I saw any London congregation; partly through the great willingness of the people, and partly by the exceeding populousness of the country, where the woods and commons are planted with nailers, scythe-smiths, and other iron labourers, like a continued village.

'When I had been but three-quarters of a year at Dudley,

I was, by God's very gracious providence, invited to Bridgnorth, the second town of Shropshire, to preach there, as assistant to the worthy pastor of that place. As soon as I heard the place described, I perceived it was the fittest for me; for there was just such employment as I desired, and could submit to, without that which I scrupled, and with some probability of peace and quietness.

'But the people proved a very ignorant, dead-hearted people, the town consisting too much of inns and ale-houses, and having no general trade to employ the inhabitants in, which is the undoing of great towns. So that though, through the great mercy of God, my first labours were not without success, to the conversion of some ignorant and careless sinners unto God, and were over-valued by those that were already regardful of the concernments of their souls, yet were they not so successful as they proved afterwards in other places. Though I was in the fervour of my affections, and never anywhere preached with more vehement desires of men's conversion, and I account my liberty with that measure of success which I there had, to be a mercy which I can never be sufficiently thankful for, yet, with the generality, an applause of the preacher was most of the success of the sermon which I could hear of; and their tippling, and ill-company, and dead-heartedness quickly drowned all.'

Though a friend to Episcopacy, yet the omission of some required ceremonies, together with his refusal to take the 'et cetera' oath, had nearly occasioned his expulsion from the ministry and the loss of his liberty, if not, in his weak and infirm state of health, of life itself. Indeed some of his accusers threatened him with 'hanging', if he did not comply. God, however, in whose hands are the hearts of all men, changed the purposes and restrained the malice of his adversaries. He continued to preach at Bridgnorth a year and three-quarters in the uninterrupted enjoyment of liberty, which, says he, 'I took to be a very great mercy to me in these troublesome times.'

He says, 'The Long Parliament, among other parts of their reformation, resolved to reform the corrupted clergy, and appointed a committee to receive petitions and complaints against them; which was no sooner understood, but multitudes in all counties came up with petitions against their ministers.

'Among all these complainers, the town of Kidder-minster in Worcestershire drew up a petition against their minister. The vicar of the place they articled against as one that was utterly insufficient for the ministry; presented by a papist; unlearned; preached but once a quarter, which was so weakly, as exposed him to laughter, and persuaded them that he understood not the very substantial article of Christianity; that he frequented ale-houses, and had sometimes been drunk; that he turned the table altar-wise, etc.; with more such as this.

'The vicar, knowing his insufficiency, and hearing how two others in this case had sped, desired to compound this business with them, which was soon accomplished. Hereupon they invited me to them from Bridgnorth. The bailiff of the town, and all the feoffees[1], desired me to preach with them, in order to a full determination. My mind was much to the place, as soon as it was described to me, because it was a full congregation, and most convenient temple; an ignorant, rude and revelling people for the greater

1. Feoff: heritable land granted by feudal lord; lord's right in such land. A feoffee was the person to whom feoff was granted.

part, who had need of preaching; and yet had among them a small company of converts, who were humble, godly and of good conversations, and not much hated by the rest, and therefore the fitter to assist their teacher: but, above all, because they had hardly ever had any lively, serious preaching among them. For Bridgnorth had made me resolve that I would never more go among a people that had been hardened in unprofitableness under an awakening ministry; but either to such as never had any convincing preacher, or to such as had profited by him.

'As soon as I came to Kidderminster, and had preached there one day, I was chosen, without opposition; for though fourteen only had the power of choosing, they desired to please the rest. And thus I was brought, by the gracious providence of God, to that place which had the chief of my labours, and yielded me the greatest fruits of comfort. And I noted the mercy of God in this, that I never went to any place in my life, among all my changes, which I had before desired, designed, or thought of, much less sought; but only to those that I never thought of, till the sudden invitation did surprise me.'

3

Kidderminster

To this important and interesting scene of labour Baxter was invited on the 9th of March, 1640. His legal appointment after labouring amongst the people during the interval, is dated April 5, 1641.

For this station of public and extensive usefulness he had been prepared by various painful and alarming afflictions. He says: 'All this forementioned time of my ministry was passed under my fore-described weaknesses, which were so great, as made me live and preach in some continual expectation of death, supposing still that I had not long to live. And this I found, through all my life, to be an invaluable mercy to me; for

'1. It greatly weakened temptations.

'2. It kept me in a great contempt of the world.

'3. It taught me highly to esteem time; so that, if any of it passed away in idleness or unprofitableness, it was so long a pain and burden to my mind. So that I must say, to the praise of my most wise Conductor, that time hath still seemed to me much more precious than gold, or any earthly gain, and its minutes have not been despised, nor have I been much tempted to any of the sins which go under the name of pastimes, since I undertook my work.

'4. It made me study and preach things necessary, and a little stirred up my sluggish heart to speak to sinners with some compassion, as a dying man to dying men.

'These, with the rest which I mentioned before, when I spake of my infirmities, were the benefits which God afforded me by affliction. I humbly bless his gracious providence, who gave me his treasure in an earthen vessel, and trained me up in the school of affliction, and taught me the cross of Christ so soon; that I might be rather, as Luther speaketh, "a cross-bearer, than a cross-maker, or imposer".'

His spiritual conflicts, too, were of a distressing character, and tended eventually, by the grace of God, to qualify him to be an instructor of others, both as a preacher and writer. He says:

'At one time, above all the rest, being under a new and unusual distemper, which put me upon the present expectations of my change, and going for comfort to the promises, as I was used, the tempter strongly assaulted my faith, and would have drawn me towards infidelity itself. Till I was ready to enter into the ministry, all my troubles had been raised by the hardness of my heart, and the doubtings of my own sincerity: but now all these began to vanish, and never much returned to this day. And, instead of these, I was now assaulted with more pernicious temptations; especially to question the certain truth of the sacred Scriptures; and also the life to come, and the immortality of the soul. And these temptations assaulted me, not as they do the melancholy, with horrid vexing importunity, but by pretence of sober reason, they would have drawn me to a settled doubting of Christianity.

'And here I found my own miscarriage, and the great mercy of God. My miscarriage, in that I had so long neglected the well settling of my foundations, while I had bestowed so much time on the superstructure and the applicatory part. For, having taken it for an intolerable evil, once to question the truth of the Scriptures and the life to come, I had either taken it for a certainty upon trust, or taken up with common reasons of it, which I had never well considered, digested, or made mine own. Insomuch, that when this temptation came, it seemed at first to answer and enervate all the former reasons of my feeble faith, which made me take the Scriptures for the word of God; and it set before me such mountains of difficulty in the incarnation, the person of Christ, his undertaking and performance, with the Scripture chronology, histories, style, etc., which had overwhelmed me, if God had not been my strength.

'And here I saw much of the mercy of God, that he let not out these terrible and dangerous temptations upon me while I was weak and in the infancy of my faith; for then I had never been able to withstand them. But faith is like a tree, whose top is small while the root is young and shallow; and, therefore, as then it hath but small rooting, so is it not liable to the shaking winds and tempests as the big and high-grown trees are; but, as the top groweth higher, so the root at once grows greater, and deeper fixed, to cause it to endure its greater assaults.

'Though formerly I was wont, when any such temptation came, to cast it aside, as fitter to be abhorred than considered of, yet now this would not give me satisfaction; but I was fain to dig to the very foundation, and seriously to examine the reasons of Christianity, and to give a hearing to all that could be said against it, that so my faith might be indeed my own. And at last I found, that "nothing is so firmly believed as that which hath been some time doubted of."

'In the storm of this temptation, I questioned awhile whether I were indeed a Christian or an infidel, and whether faith could consist with such doubts as I was conscious of. For I had read in many Papists and Protestants, that faith had certainty, and was more than an opinion; and that, if a man should live a godly life from the bare apprehensions of the probability of the truth of Scripture, and the life to come, it would not save him, as being no true godliness or faith. But my judgement closed with the reason of Dr. Jackson's determination of this case, which supported me much, that as in the very assenting act of faith there may be such weakness, as may make us cry, "Lord, increase our faith! We believe; Lord, help our belief!" so, when faith and unbelief are in their conflict, it is the effects which must show us which of them is victorious. And that he that hath so much faith as will cause him to deny himself, take up his cross, and forsake all the profits, honours, and pleasure of this world, for the sake of Christ, the love of God, and the hope of glory, hath a saving faith, how weak soever. For God cannot condemn the soul that truly loveth and seeketh him; and to those that Christ bringeth to persevere in the love of God, he bringeth salvation. And there were divers things that, in this assault, proved great assistances to my faith.

'From this assault I was forced to take notice, that it is our belief of the truth of the Word of God, and the life to come, which is the spring that sets all grace on work, and with which it rises or falls, flourishes or decays, is actuated or stands still. And, that there is more of this secret unbelief at the root than most of us are aware of; and that our love of the world, our boldness with sin, our neglect of duty, are caused hence. I observed easily in myself, that if at any time Satan did more than at other times weaken my belief of Scripture, and the life to come, my zeal in every religious duty abated with it, and I grew more indifferent in religion than before. I was more inclined to conformity in those points which I had taken to be so sinful, and was ready to think, Why should I be singular, and offend the bishops and other superiors, and make myself contemptible in the world, and expose myself to censures, scorns, and sufferings, and all for such little things as these, when the foundations themselves have such great difficulties as I am unable to overcome? But, when faith revived, then none of the parts or concerns of religion seemed small; and then man seemed nothing, and the world a shadow, and God was all.

'In the beginning I doubted not of the truth of the holy Scriptures, or of the life to come, because I saw not the difficulties which might cause doubting. After that, I saw them, and I doubted, because I saw not that which should satisfy the mind against them. Since then, having seen both difficulties and evidences, though I am not so unmolested as at the first, yet is my faith, I hope, much stronger, and far better able to repel the temptations of Satan, and the sophisms of infidels, than before. But yet it is my daily prayer that God would increase my faith, and give my soul a clear sight of the evidences of his truth, and of himself, and of the invisible world.'

Nor was Baxter exempt from the 'strife of tongues'; his moral character was assailed by base and unfounded calumnies. These he was enabled successfully to refute. His chief calumniator was obliged to confess that the charges were fabrications, and to beg his forgiveness, which was freely given.

The trials of ministers are frequently of a painful character, but, like those of private Christians, 'they work together for good.' They are over-ruled, not only for their personal benefit, but for the edification of their flocks. If their sufferings abound, so do their consolations also, and that in order to their being the comforters of others (2 Cor. 1:3-5).

Baxter entered on his work with spirit and zeal; nor was he suffered to labour long without witnessing the blessed results thereof in the conversion of sinners to God. At first, he used to register the names, characters etc. of his converts, but they became at length so numerous, that he was obliged to discontinue the practice.

He continued successfully discharging his ministerial and pastoral labours for nearly two years, when the civil wars threw the whole country into confusion. His situation, though he was no partisan, was critical and dangerous. He was at length advised by his friends to retire from Kidderminster till public affairs should assume a more peaceable aspect. The immediate occasion of his leaving he thus describes:

'About that time the Parliament sent down an order for the demolishing of all statues and images of any of the three persons in the blessed Trinity, or of the virgin Mary, which should be found in churches, or on the crosses in churchyards. My judgment was for the obeying of this order, thinking it came from just authority; but I meddled not in it, but left the churchwarden to do what he thought good. The churchwarden, an honest, sober, quiet man, seeing a crucifix upon the cross in the churchyard, set up a ladder to have reached it, but it proved too short: whilst he was gone to seek another, a crew of the drunken, riotous party of the town, poor journeymen and servants, took the alarm, and ran all together with weapons to defend the crucifix and the church images, of which there were divers left since the time of Popery.

'The report was, among them, that I was the actor, and it was me they sought; but I was walking almost a mile out of town, or else, I suppose, I had there ended my days. When they missed me and the churchwarden both, they went raving about the streets to seek us. Two neighbours, that dwelt in other parishes, hearing that they sought my life, ran in among them, to see whether I were there, and they knocked them both down in the streets; and both of them are since dead, and, I think, never perfectly recovered that hurt. When they had foamed about half an hour, and met with none of us, and were newly housed, I came in from my walk, and, hearing the people cursing at me in their doors, I wondered what the matter was, but quickly found how fairly I had escaped. The next Lord's Day I dealt plainly with them, and laid open to them the quality of that action, and told them, seeing they so requited me as to seek my blood, I was willing to leave them, and save them from that guilt. But the poor sots were so amazed and ashamed, that they took on sorrily, and were loth to part with me.

'About this time, the king's declarations were read in our market-place, and the reader, a violent country gentleman, seeing me pass the streets, stopped, and said, "There goeth a traitor," without ever giving a syllable of reason for it.

'And the commission of array was set afoot, for the Parliament meddled not with the militia of that county, the Lord Howard, their lieutenant, not appearing. Then the rage of the rioters grew greater than before! And in preparation to the war, they had got the word among them, "Down with the Roundheads!" insomuch, that in many places if a

stranger passed that had short hair and a civil habit, the
rabble presently cried, "Down with the Roundheads!" and
some they knocked down in the open streets.

'In this fury of the rabble, I was advised to withdraw
awhile from home; whereupon I went to Gloucester. As I
passed but through a corner of the suburbs of Worcester,
they that knew me not cried, "Down with the Roundheads!"
and I was glad to spur on and begone. But when I came to
Gloucester, among strangers also that had never known me,
I found a civil, courteous, and religious people, as different
from Worcester, as if they had lived under another
government.

'When I had been at Gloucester a month, my neighbours
of Kidderminster came for me home, and told me that, if I
stayed any longer, the people would interpret it, either that
I was afraid, upon some guilt, or that I was against the
king; so I bid my host, Mr. Darney, the town clerk, and my
friends, farewell, and never went to Gloucester more.

'For myself, I knew not what course to take. To live at
home I was uneasy; but especially now, when soldiers, on
one side or other, would be frequently among us, and we
must be still at the mercy of every furious beast that would
make a prey of us. I had neither money nor friends. I knew
not who would receive me in any place of safety; nor had I
anything to satisfy them for my diet and entertainment. Hereupon I was persuaded, by one that was with me, to go to
Coventry, where one of my old acquaintance was minister,
Mr. Simon King, some time schoolmaster at Bridgnorth.
So thither I went, with a purpose to stay there till one side
or other had got the victory, and the war was ended, and
then to return home again.

'Whilst I was thinking what course to take in this necessity, the committee and governor of the city desired me that I would stay with them, and lodge in the governor's house, and preach to the soldiers. The offer suited well with my necessities, but I resolved that I would not be chaplain to the regiment, nor take a commission; but, if the mere preaching of a sermon once or twice a week to the garrison would satisfy them, I would accept of the offer, till I could go home again. Here I lived, in the governor's house, and followed my studies as quietly as in a time of peace, for about a year, only preaching once a week to the soldiers, and once on the Lord's Day to the people, not taking from any of them a penny for either, save my diet only.'

The war continued with unabated fury and severity. During his stay at Coventry, he was invited by Cromwell to become chaplain to his troop which lay at Cambridge. This invitation he declined: but some time after, on learning the state of the army, and the prospects of usefulness among the soldiers, at the solicitation of Captain Evanson, he became chaplain to Colonel Whalley's regiment, and left his quarters at Coventry, to the deep and universal regret of the residents in the garrison.

On joining his regiment, he writes: 'I set myself, from day to day, to find out the corruptions of the soldiers, and to discourse and dispute them out of their mistakes, both religious and political. My life among them was a daily contending against seducers, and gently arguing with the more tractable.'

His 'efforts to do good' were unremitting. His time was occupied 'in preaching, conference, and disputing against confounding errors', and in directing and comforting believers under the difficulties and perils of the times. His success, however, did not equal his expectations: party spirit ran exceedingly high; the soldiers were divided in their religious opinions; the camp afforded but few facilities for collecting any considerable numbers together, and besides was constantly changing its position, according to the direction of war. And probably his desire to reconcile their religious differences, and to unite them under one religious discipline, led him more frequently to dispute than to preach; to dwell more on the details and minutiæ of the gospel than on its essential truths; to labour as though they were at peace and had time for punctilios, rather than as being in a state of war, and in danger every hour of being hurried into eternity. These, with other untoward circumstances, contributed to diminish the probability of success, but at the same time to illustrate the zeal, the piety, and the perseverance of the conscientious chaplain.[1]

After the fatal battle of Worcester, with health enfeebled by his excessive exertions in the army, he visited his old flock at Kidderminster, and thence proceeded to London for medical advice. His physician directed him to visit Tunbridge Wells, and try the efficacy of its waters. With this advice he complied. His health was in consequence improved, and in due time he returned to his quarters in Worcestershire, where the army still lay.

In all his peregrinations with the army and otherwise, he preached in most of the churches in the towns through which he passed. He was heard with interest and attention, but with what measure of success is unknown. No doubt can be entertained that his earnest, affectionate, and faithful preaching was attended with important results. The promise ensures success. 'My word shall not return to me void.'–

---

1. While in the army, Baxter was present at some sieges, but never was in any engagement, nor took part, personally, in any contests.

'Lo, I am with you always, even unto the end of the world.'

While quartered at the house of Sir John Cook, Melbourne, Derbyshire, he was seized with a violent bleeding at the nose, which so reduced his strength, that his case was considered almost hopeless. His countenance was so altered, as scarcely to be recognized by his most intimate friends. As soon as he could remove, he visited a friend in Leicestershire, where he remained three weeks in an exhausted state. In this state he was invited by his friends Sir Thomas and Lady Rous to take up his quarters at their mansion. Thither he was conveyed, and experienced the greatest kindness and attention. At the end of three months, having recovered his strength, he returned to Kidderminster.

During this period of sickness and retirement from public labours, he was anxious to be useful, and to be restored, if agreeable to the Divine will, that his usefulness might be increased. He states, concerning himself, 'Being conscious that my time had not been improved to the service of God as I desired it had been, I put up many an earnest prayer to God, that he would restore me, and use me more successfully in his work. And, blessed be that mercy which heard my groans in the day of my distress, and granted my desires, and wrought my deliverance, when men and means failed, and gave me opportunity to celebrate his praise.'

It was during this affliction that he wrote his justly celebrated work, *The Saints' Everlasting Rest*: a work, the usefulness of which no mortal can estimate. It was a blessing to the age in which he lived, and will continue to be so to the remotest ages of time. Had he lived only to write this work, he would not have lived in vain, and his name would have been held in 'everlasting remembrance'.

His own account of the origin and progress of the work is interesting. 'The second book which I wrote, and the first which I began, was that called *The Saints' Everlasting Rest*. Whilst I was in health, I had not the least thought of writing books, or of serving God in a more public way than preaching; but when I was weakened with great bleeding, and left solitary in my chamber, at Sir John Cook's in Derbyshire, without any acquaintance but my servant about me, and was sentenced to death by the physicians, I began to contemplate more seriously on the everlasting rest, which I apprehended myself to be just on the borders of. And that my thoughts might not too much scatter in my meditation, I began to write something on that subject, intending but the quantity of a sermon or two, which is the cause that the beginning is, in brevity and style, disproportionable to the rest; but being continued long in weakness, where I had no books, and no better employment, I followed it on till it was enlarged to the bulk in which it is published. The first three weeks I spent in it was at Mr. Nowel's house, at Kirkby Mallory, in Leicestershire; a quarter of a year more, at the seasons which so great weakness would allow, I bestowed on it at the house of Sir Thomas Rous, at Tous Lench, in Worcestershire; and I finished it, shortly after, at Kidderminster. The first and last parts were first done, being all that I intended for my own use; and the second and third parts came afterwards in, besides my first intention.

'This book it pleased God so far to bless to the profit of many, that it encouraged me to be guilty of all those writings which afterwards followed. The marginal citations I put in after I came home to my books; but almost all the book itself was written when I had no book but a Bible and a

Concordance. And I found that the transcript of the heart hath the greatest force on the hearts of others. For the good that I have heard that multitudes have received by that book, and the benefit which I have again received by their prayers, I here humbly return my thanks to Him that compelled me to write it.'

Anticipation that some objection might be made respecting its composition, he says, in his dedication of the work to the people of Kidderminster, 'It is no wonder, therefore, if I am too abrupt in the beginning, seeing I then intended but the length of a sermon or two. Much less may you wonder if the whole is very imperfect, seeing it was written, as it were, with one foot in the grave, by a man that was betwixt living and dead, that wanted strength of nature to quicken invention or affection, and had no book but his Bible, while the chief part was finished, nor had any mind of human ornaments, if he had been furnished. But oh, how sweet is this providence now to my review! which so happily forced me to the work of meditation, which I had formerly found so profitable to my soul; and showed me more mercy in depriving me of other helps than I was aware of; and hath caused my thoughts to feed on this heavenly subject, which hath more benefited me than all the studies of my life.'

On his recovery, he received a pressing invitation to return to his old charge at Kidderminster, which he instantly and cordially accepted. He was devotedly attached to his people, and considered himself bound to resist all attempts to procure his services in other places. He thus affectionately writes to 'his beloved friends':

'If either I or my labours have any public use or worth, it is wholly, though not only yours; and I am convinced, by providence, that it is the will of God it should be so. This I clearly discerned on my first coming to you, in my former abode with you, and in the time of my forced absence from you. When I was separated by the miseries of the late unhappy wars, I durst not fix in any other congregation, but lived in a military, unpleasing state, lest I should forestall my return to you, for whom I took myself reserved. The offer of great worldly accommodations, with five times the means I receive with you, was no temptation to me once to question whether I should leave you. Your free invitation of my return, your obedience to my doctrine, the strong affection I have yet towards you, above all people, and the general hearty return of love which I find from you, do all persuade me that I was sent into the world especially for the service of your souls.'

He resumed his labours under great bodily weakness, 'being seldom an hour free from pain'. He was subject to repeated attacks, from which he recovered, according to his own account, chiefly through the intercessions and fervent prayers of his friends: 'Many a time have I been brought very low, and received the sentence of death in myself, when my poor, honest, praying neighbours have met, and, upon their fasting and earnest prayers, I have recovered. Once, when I had continued weak three weeks, and was unable to go abroad, the very day that they prayed for me, being Good Friday, I recovered, and was able to preach and administer the sacrament the next Lord's Day; and was better after it, it being the first time that ever I administered it. And ever after that, whatever weakness was upon me, when I had, after preaching, administered that sacrament to many hundred people, I was much revived and eased of my infirmities.'

'Oh, how often,' he writes in his *Dying Thoughts*, 'have I cried to Him when men and means were nothing, and when no help in second causes did appear, and how often, and suddenly, and mercifully hath He delivered me! What sudden ease, what removal of long affliction have I had! Such extraordinary changes, and beyond my own and others' expectations, when many plain-hearted, upright Christians have, by fasting and prayer, sought God on my behalf, as have over and over convinced me of special providence, and that God is indeed a hearer of prayers. And wonders have I seen done for others also, upon such prayer, more than for myself: yea, and wonders for the church, and for public societies.' – 'Shall I therefore forget how often he hath heard prayers for me? and how wonderfully he often hath helped both me and others? My faith hath been helped by such experiences, and shall I forget them, or question them without cause at last?'

Baxter relates several extraordinary instances of answers to prayer, in the recovery and preservation both of himself and friends. Christians, in former days, were very attentive in seeking such blessings, and in observing such circumstances: they appear to have felt more constantly their dependence on God, and to have lived more by faith, and less by sight, than professors of our day. An old divine justly observes, 'They that watch providence shall never want a providence to watch.' At the same time we should remember, that God is to be owned in the use and success of all the means; for their efficacy is entirely from his blessing. Prayer, and the use of other means should be unitedly employed, in order that both may be successful. And when God has been pleased to answer our prayers, and to bless the means he has enabled and disposed us to employ, we must not fail gratefully to acknowledge his goodness, as the God of providence and of grace, 'who is wonderful in counsel, and excellent in working'. There is great danger, in days of comparative ease and safety, of forgetting our entire dependence on God, and the necessity of abounding in prayer. It will be one great benefit arising from Christian biography, if we are taught, by the example of our forefathers, to 'acknowledge God in all our ways'.

Having now brought down Baxter's life to the period when he settled down amongst his old friends, and resumed his accustomed labours, it will be desirable to introduce, in an abridged form, his own account of his 'employments, successes, and advantages' during his fourteen years' continuance among them.

1. Employments
'I preached, before the wars, twice each Lord's Day; but after the war, but once, and once every Thursday, besides occasional sermons.

'Every Thursday evening, my neighbours that were most desirous and had opportunity met at my house, and there one of them repeated the sermon, and afterwards they proposed what doubts any of them had about the sermon, or any other case of conscience, and I resolved their doubts. And, last of all, I caused sometimes one, and sometimes another of them to pray, to exercise them; and sometimes I prayed with them myself, which, besides singing a psalm, was all they did.

'And once a week, also, some of the younger sort, who were not fit to pray in so great an assembly, met among a few more privately, where they spent three hours in prayer together.

'Every Saturday night they met at some of their houses to repeat the sermon of the last Lord's Day, and to pray and prepare themselves for the following day.

'Once in a few weeks, we had a day of humiliation, on one occasion or other.

'Every religious woman that was safely delivered, instead of the old feastings and gossipings, if they were able, did keep a day of thanksgiving, with some of their neighbours with them, praising God, and singing psalms, and soberly feasting together.

'Two days every week, my assistant and I myself took fourteen families between us for private catechising and conference; he going through the parish, and the town coming to me. I first heard them recite the words of the catechism, and then examined them about the sense, and lastly urged them, with all possible engaging reason and vehemence, to answerable affection and practice. If any of them were perplexed, through ignorance or bashfulness, I forbore to press them any farther to answers, but made them hearers, and either examined others, or turned all into instruction and exhortation. But this I have opened more fully in my *Reformed Pastor*. I spend about an hour with a family, and admitted no others to be present, lest bashfulness should make it burdensome, or any should talk of the weakness of others. So that all the afternoons, on Mondays and Tuesdays, I spent in this, after I had begun it; for it was many years before I did attempt it; and my assistant spent the mornings of the same days in the same employment. Before that, I only catechised them in the church, and conferred with, now and then, one occasionally.

'Besides all this, I was forced, five or six years, by the people's necessity, to practise physic. A common pleurisy happening one year, and no physician being near, I was forced to advise them, to save their lives; and I could not afterwards avoid the importunity of the town and country round about. And, because I never once took a penny of any one, I was crowded with patients, so that almost twenty would be at my door at once; and though God, by more success than I expected, so long encouraged me, yet, at last, I could endure it no longer; partly because it hindered my other studies, and partly because the very fear of miscarrying and doing any one harm did make it an intolerable burden to me. So that, after some years' practice, I procured a godly, diligent physician to come and live in the town, and bound myself, by promise, to practise no more, unless in consultation with him in case of any seeming necessity. And so, with that answer I turned them all off, and never meddled with it more.'

2. Success

'I have mentioned my sweet and acceptable employment; let me, to the praise of my gracious Lord, acquaint you with some of my success. And I will not suppress it, though I foreknow that the malignant will impute the mention of it to pride and ostentation. For it is the sacrifice of thanksgiving which I owe to my most gracious God, which I will not deny him for fear of being censured as proud, lest I prove myself proud indeed, while I cannot undergo the imputation of pride in the performance of my thanks for such undeserved mercies.

'My public preaching met with an attentive, diligent auditory. Having broke over the brunt of the opposition of the rabble before the wars, I found them afterwards tractable and unprejudiced.

'Before I ever entered into the ministry, God blessed my private conference to the conversion of some, who remain firm and eminent in holiness to this day. Then, and in the beginning of my ministry, I was wont to number them as jewels; but since then I could not keep any number of them.

'The congregation was usually full, so that we were fain to build five galleries after my coming thither, the church itself being very capacious, and the most commodious and convenient that ever I was in. Our private meetings also were full. On the Lord's Day there was no disorder to be seen in the streets, but you might hear a hundred families singing psalms and repeating sermons, as you passed through the streets. In a word, when I came thither first, there was about one family in a street that worshipped God and called on his name; and when I came away, there were some streets where there was not past one family in the side of a street that did not so; and that did not, by professing serious godliness, give us hopes of their sincerity. And those families which were the worst, being inns and alehouses, usually some persons in each house did seem to be religious.

'Though our administration of the Lord's Supper was so ordered as displeased many, and the far greater part kept away themselves, yet we had six hundred that were communicants, of whom there were not twelve that I had not good hopes of, as to their sincerity; and those few that did consent to our communion, and yet lived scandalously, were excommunicated afterward. And I hope there were many that had the fear of God that came not to our communion in the sacrament, some of them being kept off by husbands, by parents, by masters, and some dissuaded by men that differed from us.

'When I set upon personal conference with each family, and catechising them, there were very few families in all the town that refused to come; and those few were beggars at the town's ends, who were so ignorant, that they were ashamed it should be manifest. And few families went from me without some tears, or seemingly serious promises for a godly life. Yet many ignorant and ungodly persons there were still among us; but most of them were in the parish, and not in the town, and in those parts of the parish which were farthest from the town.

'Some of the poor men did competently understand the body of divinity, and were able to judge in difficult controversies. Some of them were so able in prayer, that very few ministers did match them, in order and fulness, and apt expressions, and holy oratory, with fervency. Abundance of them were able to pray very laudably with their families, or with others. The temper of their minds, and the correctness of their lives, were much more laudable than their parts. The professors of serious godliness were generally of very humble minds and carriage; of meek and quiet behaviour unto others; and of blamelessness in their conversations.

'And, in my poor endeavours with my brethren in the ministry, my labours were not lost. Our disputations [discussions] proved not unprofitable; our meetings were never contentious, but always comfortable. We took great delight in the company of each other; so that I know the remembrance of those days is pleasant both to them and me. When discouragements had long kept me from motioning a way of church order and discipline, which all might agree in, that we might neither have churches ungoverned, nor fall into divisions among ourselves, at the first motioning of it I found a readier consent than I could expect, and all went on without any great obstructing difficulties. And when I attempted to bring them all conjointly to the work of catechising and instructing every family by itself, I found a ready consent in most, and performance in many.

'So that I must here, to the praise of my dear Redeemer, set up this pillar of remembrance, even to His praise who hath employed me so many years in so comfortable a work, with such encouraging success. Oh, what am I, a worthless worm, not only wanting academical honours, but much of that furniture which is needful to so high a work, that God should thus abundantly encourage me, when the reverend instructors of my youth did labour fifty years together in one place, and could scarcely say they had converted one or two of their parishioners? And the greater was this mercy, because I was naturally of a discouraged spirit; so that if I had preached one year, and seen no fruits of it, I should hardly have forborne running away like Jonah, but should have thought that God called me not to that place.'

3. Advantages

'Having related my comfortable successes in this place, I shall next tell you by what, and how many advantages this much was effected, under that grace which worketh by means, though with a free diversity; which I do for their sakes that would have the means of other men's experiments, in managing ignorant and sinful parishes.

'One advantage was, that I came to a people that never had any awakening ministry before. For if they had been hardened under a powerful ministry, and been sermon proof, I should have expected less.

'Another advantage was, that at first I was in the vigour
of my spirits, and had naturally a familiar, moving voice,
which is a great matter with the common hearers; and doing
all in bodily weakness, as a dying man, my soul was the
more easily brought to seriousness, and to preach as a dying
man to dying men; for drowsy formality and customariness
doth but stupify the hearers, and rock them asleep. It must
be serious preaching, which must make men serious in
hearing and obeying it.

'Another advantage which I had was, the acceptation of
my person. Though to win estimation and love to ourselves
only be an end that none but proud men and hypocrites
intend, yet it is most certain that the gratefulness of the
person doth ingratiate the message, and greatly prepareth
the people to receive the truth. Had they taken me to be
ignorant, erroneous, scandalous, worldly, self-seeking, or
such like, I could have expected small success among them.

'Another advantage which I had was, by the zeal and
diligence of the godly people of the place, who thirsted
after the salvation of their neighbours, and were, in private,
my assistants; and being dispersed through the town, they
were ready, in almost all companies, to repress seducing
words, and to justify godliness, and convince, reprove,
exhort men according to their needs; and also to teach them
how to pray, and to help them to sanctify the Lord's Day.
Those people that had none in their families who could
pray, or repeat the sermons, went to their next neighbour's
house who could do it, and joined with them; so that some
houses of the ablest men in each street were filled with
them that could do nothing, or little in their own.

'And the holy, humble, blameless lives of the religious
sort were a great advantage to me. The malicious people

could not say, Your professors here are as proud and covetous as any. But the blameless lives of godly people did shame opposers, and put to silence the ignorance of foolish men, and many were won by their good conversation.

'Our private meetings were a marvellous help to the propagating of godliness among them; for thereby truths that slipped away were recalled, and the seriousness of the people's minds renewed, and good desires cherished; and hereby their knowledge was much increased; and here the younger sort learned to pray, by frequently hearing others. And here I had opportunity to know their case; for, if any were touched and awakened in public, I should presently see them drop in to our private meetings.

'Another furtherance of my work was the writings which I wrote, and gave among them. Some small books I gave each family one of, which came to about eight hundred, and of the bigger I gave fewer; and every family that was poor, and had not a Bible, I gave a Bible to. And I had found myself the benefit of reading to be so great, that I could not but think it would be profitable to others.

'And it was a great advantage to me, that my neighbours were of such a trade as allowed them time enough to read or talk of holy things; for the town liveth upon the weaving of Kidderminster stuffs, and, as they stand in their loom, they can set a book before them, or edify one another.

'And I found that my single life afforded me much advantage; for I could the more easily take my people for my children, and think all that I had too little for them, in that I had no children of my own to tempt me to another way of using it. And being discharged from the most of family cares, keeping but one servant, I had the greater vacancy and liberty of the labours of my calling.

'And God made use of my practice of physic among them, as a very great advantage to my ministry; for they that cared not for their souls, did love their lives, and care for their bodies. And by this they were made almost as observant as a tenant is of his landlord. Sometimes I could see before me in the church a very considerable part of the congregation, whose lives God had made me a means to save, or to recover their health; and doing it for nothing so obliged them, that they would readily hear me.

'And it was a great advantage to me, that there were at last a few that were bad, but some of their own relations were converted. Many children did God work upon at fourteen, or fifteen, or sixteen years of age; and this did marvellously reconcile the minds of the parents and elder sort to godliness. They that would not hear me, would hear their own children. They that before could have talked against godliness, would not hear it spoken against when it was their children's case. Many that would not be brought to themselves, were proud that they had understanding, religious children. And we had some old persons, of near eighty years of age, who are, I hope, in heaven, and the conversion of their own children was the chief means to overcome their prejudices, and old customs, and conceits.

'And God made great use of sickness to do good to many. For though sick-bed promises are usually soon forgotten, yet was it otherwise with many among us; and, as soon as they were recovered, they first came to our private meetings, and so kept in a learning state, till further fruits of piety appeared.

'Another of my great advantages was the true worth and unanimity of the honest ministers of the country around about us, who associated in a way of concord with us. Their preaching was powerful and sober; their spirits peaceable and meek, disowning the treasons and iniquities of the times as well as we; they were wholly addicted to the winning of souls; self-denying, and of most blameless lives; evil spoken of by no sober men, but greatly beloved by their own people, and all that knew them; adhering to no faction; neither episcopal, presbyterian, nor independent, as to parties; but desiring union, and loving that which is good in all.

'Another great help to my success at last, was the before described work of personal conference with every family apart, and catechising and instructing them. That which was spoken to them personally, and put them sometimes upon answers, awakened their attention, and was more easily applied than public preaching, and seemed to do much more upon them.

'And the exercise of church discipline was no small furtherance of the people's good; for I found plainly, that without it I could not have kept the religious sort from separations and divisions. There is something generally in their dispositions, which inclineth them to dissociate from open ungodly sinners, as men of another nature and society; and if they had not seen me do something reasonable for a regular separation of the notorious obstinate sinners from the rest, they would have withdrawn themselves irregularly; and it would have been in my power, with bare words, to satisfy them, when they saw we had liberty to do what we would.

'Another advantage which I found to my success, was by ordering my doctrine to them in a suitableness to the main end, and yet so as might suit their dispositions and diseases. The thing which I daily opened to them, and with greatest importunity laboured to imprint upon their minds, was the great fundamental principles of Christianity, even a right knowledge and belief of, and subjection and love to, God the Father, the Son, and the Holy Ghost; and love to all men, and concord with the church and one another. I did so daily inculcate the knowledge of God our Creator, Redeemer, and Sanctifier, and love and obedience to God, and unity with the church catholic, and love to men, and hope of life eternal, that these were the matter of their daily cogitations and discourses, and indeed their religion. And yet I did usually put something in my sermon which was above their own discovery, and which they had not known before; and this I did, that they might be kept humble, and still perceive their ignorance, and be willing to keep in a learning state. And I did this also to increase their knowledge, and also to make religion pleasant to them, by a daily addition to their former light, and to draw them on with desire and delight. But these things which they did not know before were not unprofitable controversies which tended not to edification, nor novelties in doctrine contrary to the universal church; but either such points as tended to illustrate the great doctrines before mentioned, or usually about the right methodizing of them: as the opening of the true and profitable method of the creed or doctrine of faith, the Lord's prayer or matter of our desires, and the ten commandments or law of practice; which afford matter to add to the knowledge of most professors of religion a long time. And when that is done, they must be led on still further by degrees, as they are capable, but so as not to leave the weak behind; and so shall be truly subservient to the great points of faith, hope, and love, holiness and unity, which must be still inculcated as the beginning and the end of all.

'And it much furthered my success, that I stayed still in this one place, near two years before the wars, and above fourteen years after; for he that removeth often from place to place may sow good seeds in many places, but is not likely to see much fruits in any, unless some other skilful hand shall follow him to water it. It was a great advantage to me to have almost all the religious people of the place of my own instructing and informing; and that they were not formed into erroneous and factious principles before; and that I stayed to see them grown up to some confirmedness and maturity.'

These passages strikingly depict the means and effects of a revival of religion; and surely there is nothing so impracticable in those means as to preclude the hope that they may be employed by others, and with similar, if not equal results. Only let love to the Redeemer burn with quenchless ardour in the breast, and eternity with its tremendous and unutterable consequences be distinctly realized; compassion to immortal spirits infuse its tenderness and solicitude throughout the soul; a deep and unfailing sense of ministerial responsibility rest upon the conscience; then all the powers, talents, and influence that can be commanded will be brought into exercise, and made to bear with unceasing energy on the great work of saving immortal souls, and then the Lord will command his 'blessing, even life for evermore'.

Importance of winning young people

Probably, the chief defect in modern ministerial duties has been in confining the attention too much to the pulpit, and not sufficiently attending to the interests of the young. A considerable improvement in both these respects has of late taken place, and great good may be expected to result. The secret of Baxter's success lay in the zeal, affection, and perseverance he displayed in following his people to their homes. His visits from house to house were for the purpose of applying, with more close and pungent force, the truths which were taught from the pulpit, or learned in the systematic instructions which were given to families and to children. And it is remarkable, that his success in the earliest period of his ministry was chiefly amongst the young. In the preface to his work, entitled *Compassionate Counsel to all Young Men*, he observes:

'In the place where God most blessed my labours at Kidderminster, my first and greatest success was upon the youth; and which was a marvellous way of divine mercy when God had touched the hearts of young men and girls with a love of goodness, and delightful obedience to the truth, the parents and grandfathers, who had grown old in an ignorant and worldly state, did fall into a liking and love of piety, induced by the love of their children, whom they perceived to be made by it much wiser and better, and more dutiful to them.'

'By much experience I have been made more sensible of the necessity of warning and instructing youth than I was before. The sad reports of fame have taught it to me; the sad complaints of mournful parents have taught it me; the sad observation of the wilful impenitence of some of my acquaintance tells it me; the many scores, if not hundreds of bills, that have been publicly put up to me to pray for wicked and obstinate children have told it me; and, by the grace of God, the penitent confessions, lamentations, and restitutions of many converts have made me more particularly acquainted with their case; which moved me, on my Thursday's lecture, awhile to design the first of every month to speak to youth, and those that educate them.'

The religious education of youth is of infinite importance to families and to a nation; to the church and the world.

The youthful members of his congregation should engage the anxious attention of every pastor. They are the hopes of his ministry. With them truth meets the readiest reception. Amongst them conversion most frequently takes place. From them the most valuable members of Christian society are obtained. Rising into life, their influence is exerted wholly on the side of truth and piety; and, when more matured in years, their instructions and example benefit and bless their families, their connections, and the world. The salvation of one soul in the period of youth prevents its entering on a course of sin, engages it to the practices of holiness, ensures the exertion of its influence in behalf of God and his cause through the whole of its earthly being; and thus a career of happiness begins, which shall extend throughout eternity.

The Reformed Pastor

In connection with this statement of Baxter's labours and success, some notice may be taken of his work entitled *The Reformed Pastor*, written expressly to arouse the attention and excite the efforts of the Christian ministry to the great work in which he himself had so successfully engaged. His reverend brethren had witnessed the

astonishing results of his pastoral engagements, and were
anxious to make some efforts to accomplish in their own
parishes a similar result. A day of fasting and prayer was
appointed by themselves at Worcester, before entering on
their untried labours, and Baxter was requested to preach
on the occasion. He prepared his sermon, but his illness
prevented his preaching. He therefore enlarged his sermon
into a treatise, and published it under the title of *Gildas
Salvianus.* Concerning this work he says:

'I have very great cause to be thankful to God for the
success of that book, as hoping many thousand souls are
the better for it, in that it prevailed with many ministers to
set upon that work which I there exhort them to. Even from
beyond the seas I have had letters of request, to direct them
how they might bring on that work, according as that book
had convinced them that it was their duty. If God would
but reform the ministry, and set them on their duties
zealously and faithfully, the people would certainly be
reformed. All churches either rise or fall as the ministry
doth rise or fall, not in riches and worldly grandeur, but in
knowledge, zeal, and ability for their work.'

Many and just encomiums have been passed on this
work. 'In the whole compass of divinity there is scarcely
anything superior to it, in close, pathetic appeals to the
conscience of the minister of Christ, upon the primary duties
of his office.'

The editor of a recent edition justly says: 'Of the
excellence of this work, it is scarcely possible to speak in
too high terms. For powerful, pathetic, pungent, and heart-
piercing address, we know of no work on the pastoral care
to be compared with it. Could we suppose it to be read by
an angel, or by some other being possessed of an unfallen

nature, the argumentation and expostulations of our author would be felt to be altogether irresistible: and hard must be the heart of that minister who can read it without being moved, melted, and overwhelmed; hard must be his heart, if he be not roused to greater faithfulness, diligence, and activity, in winning souls to Christ. It is a work worthy of being printed in letters of gold. It deserves, at least, to be engraven on the heart of every minister.'

To this recommendation may be subjoined his advice to the more wealthy followers of Christ: 'I cannot help suggesting to the friends of religion that they could not, perhaps, do more good at less expense, than be presenting copies of this work to the ministers of Christ throughout the country. They are the chief instruments through whom good is to be effected in any country. How important, then, must it be to stir them up to holy zeal and activity in the cause of the Redeemer! A tract given to a poor man may be the means of his conversion; but a work, such as this, presented to a minister, may, through his increased faithfulness and energy, prove the conversion of multitudes.'

In addition to Baxter's numerous ministerial and pastoral labours, he was consulted by persons of all classes and professions on the various subjects connected with church and state, which at that period were hotly and fiercely agitated. His pacific disposition, and his desire to promote universal concord among all religious parties, were generally known. Hence his advice was eagerly sought by all. This must have occupied no small portion of his time, and caused him no little anxiety. He gives a curious account of his being consulted by Cromwell, and his preaching before him.

'At this time Lord Broghill and the Earl of Warwick

brought me to preach before Cromwell, the Protector, which was the only time that ever I preached to him, save once long before, when he was an inferior man, among other auditors. I knew not which way to provoke him better to his duty, than be preaching on 1 Corinthians 1:10, against the divisions and distractions of the church, and showing how mischievous a thing it was for politicians to maintain such divisions for their own ends, that they might fish in troubled waters, and keep the church by its divisions in a state of weakness, lest it should be able to offend them; and to show the necessity and means of union. But the plainness and nearness I heard was displeasing to him and his courtiers; but they put it up.

'A while after, Cromwell sent to speak with me; and when I came, in the presence only of three of his chief men, he began a long and tedious speech to me of God's providence in the change of the government, and how God had owned it, and what great things had been done at home and abroad, in the peace with Spain and Holland etc. When he had wearied us all with speaking thus slowly about an hour, I told him it was too great condescension to acquaint me so fully with all these matters which were above me, but I told him that we took our ancient monarchy to be a blessing, and not an evil to the land, and humbly craved his patience that I might ask him how England had ever forfeited that blessing, and unto whom the forfeiture was made? I was fain to speak of the species of government only, for they had lately made it treason by a law to speak for the person of the king. Upon that question he was awakened into some passion, and told me it was no forfeiture, but God had changed it as pleased him; and then he let fly at the parliament, which thwarted him; and especially by name at four or five of those members who were my chief acquaintance; and I presumed to defend them against his passion, and thus four or five hours were spent.

'A few days after, he sent for me again, to hear my judgment about liberty of conscience, which he pretended to be most zealous for, before almost all his privy council, where, after another slow, tedious speech of his, I told him a little of my judgment.'

Baxter was also consulted by various private individuals on cases of conscience, which he was requested to solve. To these parties he lent a willing ear, and administered suitable advice; or he replied to them in suitable and interesting letters. This must have occupied his time considerably. Besides, during his residence at Kidderminster, and while pursuing his indefatigable labours amongst his flock, he wrote and published nearly sixty different works, many of them quarto volumes of considerable size. Among these may be specially enumerated, in addition to those already noticed, his *Call to the Unconverted, A Treatise on Conversion, On Self-denial,* on *Crucifying the World,* on *Peace of Conscience,* as well as others.

These herculean labours seem incredible. But for the existence of the works themselves, his own declarations, and the concurring testimony of his several biographers, it would have been deemed impossible that, with his enfeebled health and incessant pain, he could have accomplished so much in so small a space of time.

His own account of his general labours shows at once the piety and devotedness, the spirit and energy, the zeal and perseverance of this most extraordinary man. He remarks:

'But all these my labours, except my private conferences with the families, even preaching and preparing for it, were but my recreations, and, as it were, the work of my spare hours; for my writings were my chief daily labour, which yet went the more slowly on, that I never one hour had an amanuensis to dictate to, and especially because by weakness took up so much of my time. For all the pains that my infirmities ever brought upon me were never half so grievous an affliction to me, as the unavoidable loss of my time which they occasioned.'

His treatise on *Self-denial* originated in his deep conviction of the 'breadth, and length, and depth of the radical, universal, odious sin of selfishness'. Under this conviction he preached a series of sermons on the subject, and, at the urgent entreaty of his friends, he published them in the form they now assume. He says, that the work 'found better acceptance than most of his other, but yet prevented not the ruin of church and state, and millions of souls by that sin'.

Previously to this he had published his work on *Conversion*, which, he says, 'was taken from plain sermons which Mr. Baldwin had transcribed out of my notes. And though I had no leisure for this or other writings, to take much care of the style, nor to add any ornaments or citations of authors, I thought it might better pass as it was, than not at all; and that if the author missed of the applause of the learned, yet the book might be profitable to the ignorant, as it proved, through the great mercy of God.'

Apologizing for the plainness and earnestness of his manner, he observes: 'The commonness and the greatness of men's necessity commanded me to do anything that I could for their relief, and to bring forth some water to cast upon this fire, though I had not at hand a silver vessel to carry it in, nor thought it the most fit. The plainest words are the most profitable oratory in the weightiest matters. Fineness is for ornament, and delicacy for delight; but they answer not necessity, though sometimes they may modestly attend that which answers it. Yea, when they are conjunct, it is hard for the necessitous hearer or reader to observe the matter of ornament and delicacy, and not to be carried from the matter of necessity; and to hear or read a neat, concise sententious discourse, and not to be hurt by it; for it usually hindereth the due operation of the matter, keeps it from the heart, stops it in the fancy, and makes it seem as light as the style. We use not to stand upon compliment, when we run to quench a common fire, nor to call men to escape from it by an eloquent speech. If we see a man fall into fire or water, we stand not upon mannerliness in plucking him out, but lay hands upon him as we can without delay.'

Baxter's *Call to the Unconverted* was made remarkably useful. He says:

'The occasion of this was my converse with Bishop Usher, while I was at London, who, much approving my method of directions for peace of conscience, was importunate with me to write directions suited to the various states of Christians, and also against particular sins. I reverenced the man, but disregarded these persuasions, supposing I could do nothing but what is done as well or better already. But when he was dead, his words went deeper to my mind, and I purposed to obey his counsel; yet so as that to the first sort of men, the ungodly, I thought vehement persuasions meeter than directions only. And so for such I published this little book, which God hath blessed with unexpected success beyond all the rest that I have written, except the *Saints' Rest*. In a little more than a year there were about twenty thousand of them printed by my own consent, and about ten thousand since, besides many thousands by stolen impressions, which poor men stole for lucre's sake. Through God's mercy I have had information of almost whole households converted by this small book which I set so light by. And as if all this in England, Scotland, and Ireland, were not mercy enough to me, God, since I was silenced, hath sent it over on his message to many beyond the seas; for when Mr. Eliot had printed all the Bible in the Indians' language, he next translated this my *Call to the Unconverted*, as he wrote to us here.'

In addition to its usefulness mentioned by Baxter himself, Dr. Bates relates an instance of six brothers being converted at one time by this invaluable book. To this work, distinguished for its cogent arguments, its powerful appeals, its intense and impassioned earnestness, its melting pathos, multitudes not in glory, and many advancing thither, stand indebted for their first serious impressions. Urged by its awful denunciations, they have fled from the 'city of destruction'; they have sought refuge at the cross of Calvary. Like the preaching of John, it is the precursor of the gospel: it awakens, alarms, and terrifies only that it may lead to peace, holiness, and glory through Christ.

Among other methods of doing good, Baxter adopted the plan which is now so generally employed, namely, that of publishing small tracts, broad-sheets, or hand-bills. He published various broad-sheets, and had them affixed to walls and public buildings, that the attention of passengers might be arrested, and that those who had no leisure for larger works, or were indisposed to purchase treatise, might be informed, edified, and saved. This plan he adopted with great success during the raging of the plague.

This was certainly the most active, useful, and important period of his life. His labours subsequently to this were of a more chequered, desultory, and less obvious character. Their results, though undoubtedly great, inasmuch as he laboured with the same zeal, piety, and devotedness as heretofore, yet could not be perceived so manifestly as when his efforts were concentrated in one spot, and were superintended by his untiring pastoral vigilance. The time of persecution for conscience' sake was at hand. He therefore, in common with multitudes of his brethren, was obliged to labour in such places, and on such occasions only, as the providence of God pointed out. But these labours were not in vain, for, as in days of old, they 'that were scattered abroad went everywhere preaching the gospel.'

4

Restoration of the Monarchy

Baxter had acquired great celebrity, both as a preacher and writer. He was known, moreover, to be an ardent friend to civil and ecclesiastical peace. Hence he was frequently consulted on these subjects, not only by ministers, but by the higher powers. On various occasions he went to London, and it would seem chiefly on business relating both to the church and the nation. Early in April, 1660, he left Kidderminster, and reached London on the 13th of that month. The reason of his leaving is not stated, but it appears evidently to have been in connection with the state of public affairs.

It was a saying of Baxter's, that we are 'no more choosers of our employments than of our successes'. The truth of this observation he was now called to verify by his own experience. On reaching London, he was consulted on the subject of the 'Restoration'. This event he, in common with multitudes of his brethren, was desirous of seeing accomplished.

The new parliament appointed a day of fasting and prayer, and required Baxter to preach before them on the occasion. This occurred the day before the bill was passed for the return of the exiled monarch. Shortly after, he was called to preach a thanksgiving sermon, on Monk's success, at St. Paul's, before the Lord Mayor and aldermen. Neither of the sermons appears to have given entire satisfaction.

His moderate views displeased partisans of all sides: some charged him with sedition; others with vacillation and temporizing in politics. He was, however, friend to the king, and rejoiced in the prospect of his restoration. He used all his efforts to promote its accomplishment, though not without fears as to the final results.

When King Charles was restored, amid the general acclamations of the nation, several of the Presbyterian ministers were made chaplains in ordinary to him, amongst whom was Baxter. His certificate of appointment to the office is dated June 26, 1660. Various conferences were held by Baxter and his friends, to promote a union between Episcopacy and Presbyterianism. A meeting was held on the subject, in the presence of Charles, at which Baxter was the chief speaker. His address on the occasion is distinguished alike by its piety and fidelity. He was desirous of promoting and securing the religious liberties of the people, and of preventing those measures which he perceived were contemplated to remove many of the most holy and zealous preachers from their flocks. The following passage from his address to the king shows the efforts that had been made to preserve the gospel ministry during the commonwealth, and his desire that, under the dominion of their rightful monarch, the same invaluable privilege might be preserved.

'I presumed to tell him (his majesty) that the people we spake for were such as were contented with an interest in heaven, and the liberty and advantages of the gospel to promote it; and if this were taken from them, and they were deprived of their faithful pastors, and liberty of worshipping God, they would take themselves undone in this world, whatever plenty else they should enjoy; and the hearts of

his most faithful subjects, who hope for his help, would
even be broken; and that we doubted not but his majesty
desired to govern a people made happy by him, and not a
broken-hearted people, that took themselves to be undone,
by the loss of that which is dearer to them than all the
riches in the world. And I presumed to tell him, That the
late usurpers that were over us so well understood their
own interest, that, to promote it, they had found the way of
doing good to be the most effectual means, and had placed
and encouraged many thousand faithful ministers in the
church, even such as detested their usurpation. And so far
had they attained their ends hereby, that it was the principal
means of their interest in the people, and the good opinion
that any had conceived of them; and those of them that had
taken the contrary course had thereby broken themselves
to pieces. Wherefore I humbly craved his majesty's patience
that we might have the freedom to request of him, that, as
he was our lawful king, in whom all his people, save a
few inconsiderable persons, were prepared to centre, as
weary of their divisions, and glad of the satisfactory means
of union in him, so he would be pleased to undertake this
blessed work of promoting their holiness and concord; for
it was not faction or disobedience which we desired him
to indulge. And that he would never suffer himself to be
tempted to undo the good which Cromwell or any other
had done, because they were usurpers that did it, or
discountenance a faithful ministry, because his enemies had
set them up. But that he would rather outgo them in doing
good, and opposing and rejecting the ignorant and ungodly,
of what opinion or party soever. For the people, whose
cause we recommended to him, had their eyes on him, as
the officer of God, to defend them in the possession of the

helps of their salvation; which, if he were pleased to vouchsafe them, their estates and lives would be cheerfully offered to his service.

'The king gave us not only a free audience, but as gracious an answer as we could expect; professing his gladness to hear our inclinations to agreement, and his resolution to do his part to bring us together: and that it must not be by bringing one party over to the other, but by abating somewhat on both sides, and meeting in the midway; and that, if it were not accomplished, it should be of ourselves, and not of him: nay, that he was resolved to see it brought to pass, and that he would draw us together himself: with some more to this purpose. Insomuch, that old Mr. Ash burst out into tears with joy, and could not forbear expressing what gladness this promise of his majesty had put into his heart.'

Proposals of agreement were submitted to the king and his advisers, but without effect. Subsequently to this, Baxter was offered a bishopric by the Lord Chancellor, but this, for various reasons of expediency, he declined. He did not consider it 'as a thing unlawful in itself,' but he thought he 'could better serve the church without it'. In the letter, in which he declines episcopal honours, he begs of the Lord Chancellor that he might be allowed to preach to his old charge at Kidderminster. He says:

'When I had refused a bishopric, I did it on such reasons as offended not the Lord Chancellor; and, therefore, instead of it, I presumed to crave his favour to restore me to preach to my people at Kidderminster again, from whence I had been cast out, when many hundreds of others were ejected, upon the restoration of all them that had been sequestered. It was but a vicarage, and the vicar was a poor, unlearned,

ignorant, silly reader, that little understood what Christianity
and the articles of his creed did signify; but once a quarter
he said something which he called a sermon, which made
him the pity or laughter of the people. This man, being
unable to preach himself, kept always a curate under him
to preach. Before the wars I had preached there only as a
lecturer, and he was bound in a bond of £500 to pay me
£60 per annum, and afterward he was sequestered, as is
before sufficiently declared. My people were so dear to
me, and I to them, that I would have been with them upon
the lowest lawful terms. Some laughed at me for refusing a
bishopric, and petitioning to be a reading vicar's curate.
But I had little hopes of so good a condition, at least for
any considerable time.'

His application, however, proved unsuccessful; for
arrangements could not be made between the patron and
the Chancellor respecting the removal of the old vicar, who
retained the charge of four thousand souls, though utterly
incompetent for his important duties, and Baxter was left
without a cure.

Missionary emphasis of his ministry
Though not permitted to return to his charge, he nevertheless
exerted himself in various ways to promote the glory of
God, and the good of souls. His attention was, at this period,
drawn to the subject of missions among the North American
Indians. Eliot, the 'Apostle of the Indians', and his
assistants, had effected much good among the roving tribes
of America. Cromwell had entered warmly into the cause,
and ordered collections to be made in every parish for the
propagation of the gospel in those distant regions. Funds
were raised, a society was formed and incorporated, and

much good was effected. At the Restoration some parties, inimical to the truth, endeavoured to destroy the institution, and to appropriate the funds to other objects. Baxter, assisted by others, exerted himself to prevent this spoliation [pillage]; and, by his influence at court, succeeded in securing the property, and in restoring the society to its original design.

For his exertions, he received a letter of thanks from the governor of New England, and another from the venerable Eliot. The latter informs Baxter of his intention to translate the *Call to the Unconverted* into the Indian language, but waited for his permission, his counsel, and his prayers. To this letter Baxter replied. A few extracts from his reply will show the interest that both he and many others felt in the cause of missions in those troublous times.

'Reverend and much honoured brother,

'Though our sins have separated us from the people of our love and care, and deprived us of all public liberty of preaching the gospel of our Lord, I greatly rejoice in the liberty, help, and success which Christ hath so long vouchsafed you in this work. There is no man on earth whose work I think more honourable and comfortable than yours. To propagate the gospel and kingdom of Christ unto those dark parts of the world, is a better work than our hating and devouring one another. There are many here that would be ambitious of being your fellow-labourers, but that they are informed you have access to no greater a number of the Indians than you yourself and your present assistants are able to instruct. An honourable gentleman, Mr. Robert Boyle, the governor of the corporation for your work, a man of great learning and worth, and of a very public, universal mind, did motion to me a public collection in all our churches, for the maintaining of such ministers as are willing to go hence to you, partly while they are learning the Indian language, and partly while they after labour in the work, as also to transport them. But I find those backward to it that I have spoke to about it, partly suspecting it a design of those that would be rid of them (but, if it would promote the work of God, this objection were too carnal to be regarded by good men); partly fearing that when the money is gathered, the work may be frustrated by the alienation of it, but this I think they need not fear, so far as to hinder any; partly because they think there will be nothing considerable gathered, because the people that are unwillingly divorced from their teachers will give nothing to send them farther from them, and those that are willingly separated from them will give nothing to those they no more respect; but specially because they think, on the aforesaid grounds, that there is no work for them to do if they were with you. There are many here, I conjecture, that would be glad to go any whither, to Persians, Tartarians, Indians, or any unbelieving nation, to propagate the gospel, if they thought they could be serviceable; but the defect of their languages is their great discouragement.

'The industry of the Jesuits and friars, and their successes in Congo, Japan, China etc., shame us all, save you. But yet, for their personal labours in the work of the gospel, here are many that would be willing to lay out, where they have liberty and a call, though scarce any that will do more in furthering great and public works. I should be glad to learn from you how far your Indian tongue extendeth; how large or populous the country is that useth it, if it be known and whether it reach only to a few scattered neighbours, who cannot themselves convey their knowledge far because of other languages. We very much rejoice in your happy work, the translation of the Bible, and bless God that hath strengthened you to finish it. If anything of mine may be honoured to contribute in the least measure to your blessed work, I shall have great cause to be thankful to God, and wholly submit the alteration and use of it to your wisdom.'

The state of the heathen appears to have occupied the thoughts of Baxter through the whole course of his ministry. Numerous allusions and references to the subject are found in his writings. In the preface to his work entitled the *Reasons of the Christian Religion*, he states that his desire to promote 'the conversion of idolaters and infidels to God and the Christian faith', was one of the reasons which prompted him to write that work. 'The doleful thought, that five parts of the world were still heathens and Mohammedans, and that Christian princes and preachers did no more for their recovery,' awakened the most painful anxiety and distress in his mind. In his work, *How to do good to many*, he asks, 'Is it not possible at least to help the poor ignorant Armenians, Greeks, Muscovites, and other Christians who have no printing among them, nor much preaching and knowledge; and, for want of printing, have very few Bibles, even for their churches or minister? Could nothing be done to get some Bibles, catechisms, and practical books printed in their own tongues, and given among them? I know there is difficulty in the way; but money, and willingness, and diligence might do something. Might not something be done in other plantations, as well as in New England, towards the conversion of the natives there? Might not some skilful, zealous preacher be sent thither, who would promote serious piety among those of the English that have too little of it, and might invite the

Americans to learn the gospel, and teach our planters how
to behave themselves Christianly towards them, to win them
to Christ?'

How powerfully affecting, and yet how truly applicable,
even at the present hour, is the following passage contained
in his life!

'It would make a believer's heart to bleed, if anything
in the world will do it, to think that five parts in six of the
world are still heathens, Mohammedans, and infidels, and
that the wicked lives of Christians, with fopperies, ignorance,
and divisions, is the great impediment to their conversion! To
read and hear travellers and merchants tell that the Banians,
and other heathens in Hindostan, Cambaia, and many other
lands, and the Mohammedans adjoining to the Greeks, and
the Abyssinians etc., do commonly fly from Christianity,
and say, "God will not save us if we be Christians, for
Christians are drunkards, and proud, and deceivers." And
that the Mohammedans and many heathens have more, both
of devotion and honesty, than the common sort of Christians
have that live among them! Oh wretched Christians! that
are not content to damn themselves, but thus lay stumbling-
blocks before the world! It were better for these men that
they had never been born! But, if all these notorious ones
were disowned by the churches, it would quit our
profession much from the dishonour, and show poor infidels
that our religion is good, though their lives be bad.'

At the close of his life, and on the near approach of
eternity, his mind was deeply interested on this important
subject. The unbounded benevolence of his heart is poured
forth in the following extract from his solemn review of
his own character, made in his last days:

'My soul is much more afflicted with the thoughts of the

miserable world, and more drawn out in desire of their conversion than heretofore. I was wont to look but little farther than England in my prayers, as not considering the state of the rest of the world; or, if I prayed for the conversion of the Jews, that was almost all. But now, as I better understand the case of the world, and the method of the Lord's Prayer, so there is nothing in the world that lieth so heavy upon my heart, as the thought of the miserable nations of the earth. It is the most astonishing part of all God's providence to me, that he so far forsaketh almost all the world, and confineth his special favour to so few; that so small a part of the world hath the profession of Christianity, in comparison of heathens, Mohammedans, and other infidels! and that, among professed Christians, there are so few that are saved from gross delusions, and have any competent knowledge; and that, among those, there are so few that are seriously religious, and truly set their hearts on heaven. I cannot be affected so much with the calamities of my own relations, or the land of my nativity, as with the case of the heathen, Mohammedan, and ignorant nations of the earth. No part of my prayers is so deeply serious, as that for the conversion of the infidel and ungodly world, that God's name may be sanctified, and his kingdom come, and his will be done on earth, as it is in heaven. Nor was I ever before so sensible what a plague the division of languages was, which hindereth our speaking to them for their conversion; nor what a great sin tyranny is, which keepeth out the gospel from most of the nations of the world. Could we but go among Tartars, Turks, and heathens, and speak their language, I should be but little troubled for the silencing of eighteen hundred ministers at once in England, nor for all the rest that were cast out here, and in Scotland

and Ireland. There being no employment in the world so desirable in my eyes, as to labour for the winning of such miserable souls, which maketh me greatly honour Mr. John Eliot, the apostle of the Indians in New England, and whoever else have laboured in such work.'

Baxter almost despaired of the conversion of the world. The obstacles to missionary enterprise were at that time insurmountable. 'He that surveyeth the present state of the earth,' he writes to his friend Eliot, 'and considereth that scarcely a sixth part is Christian, and how small a part of them have much of the power of godliness, will be ready to think that Christ hath called almost all his chosen, and is ready to forsake the earth, rather than that he intendeth us such blessed days as we desire.'

But 'what hath God wrought!' How great the change in the state of religion, both at home and abroad, since the days of Baxter! Persecution has fled; religion has revived; the missionary spirit has been enkindled; prayer has been offered; money has been poured into the coffers of the sanctuary; commerce has presented facilities for introducing the gospel into all parts of the earth; wide and effectual doors have been opened; missionaries have gone forth to the help of the Lord against the mighty, and great success has attended their labours: so that we are evidently approaching nearer to the period when the proclamation shall be made, 'The kingdoms of this world are become the kingdoms of our Lord, and of his Christ; and he shall reign for ever and ever' (Rev. 11:15).

Persecution increases

About this period the celebrated Savoy Conference was held. The object was to effect a reconciliation between the different religious parties, that they might be united in one common profession of Christianity. At this conference Baxter took a prominent part. He was sincerely desirous for the peace of the church, and that an accommodation should ensue. For this purpose he submitted various propositions, but without effect: and after some weeks' deliberations the conference was broken up, without the least hope or possibility, under existing circumstances, either of comprehension or reconciliation. Baxter was charged by his antagonists with 'speaking too boldly, and too long'; but this he accounted not a crime, but a virtue. 'I thought it a cause I could comfortably suffer for, and should as willingly be a martyr for charity as for faith.'

This was the last public and authorized attempt to promote peace and unity by argument and persuasion. Thenceforwards other measures were tried to effect so desirable an object, and, by consequence, the divergence of the parties became greater than ever.

From the termination of the Savoy Conference, the case of the dissidents became more trying and perplexing. They were calumniated, and charged with preaching sedition, or with forming plots against the government. Baxter, whose loyalty was unimpeachable, and whose ruling passion was a desire for peace, whose very soul was love, appears to have been particularly marked as an object for the shafts of calumny. He says:

'So vehement was the endeavour in court, city and country to make me contemptible and odious, as if the authors had thought that the safety either of church or state did lie upon it, and all would have been safe if I were but vilified and hated. So that any stranger that had but heard and seen all this, would have asked, "What monster of villany is this man? and what is the wickedness that he is guilty of?" Yet was I never questioned to this day before a magistrate. Nor do my adversaries charge me with any personal wrong to them; nor did they ever accuse me of any heresy, nor much contemn my judgment, nor ever accuse my life, but for preaching where another had been sequestered that was an insufficient reader, and for preaching to the soldiers of the parliament; though none of them knew my business there, nor the service that I did them. These are all the crimes, besides my writings, that I ever knew they charged my life with.

'Though no one accused me of anything, nor spake a word to me of it, being (they knew I had long been) near a hundred miles off, yet did they defame me all over the land, as guilty of a plot; and when men were taken up and sent to prison, in other counties, it was said to be for Baxter's plot: so easy was it, and so necessary a thing it seemed then, to cast such filth upon my name.

'And though, through the great mercy of God, I had long been learning not to overvalue the thoughts of men, no, not so much as the reputation of honesty or innocency, yet I was somewhat wearied with this kind of life, to be every day calumniated, and hear new slanders raised of me, and court and country ring of that which no man ever mentioned to my face: and I was often thinking to go beyond sea, that I might find some place in retired privacy to live and end my days in quietness, out of the noise of a peace-hating generation. But my acquaintance thought I might be more serviceable here, though there I might live more in quietness; and having not the vulgar language of any country, to enable me to preach to them, or converse with them, and being so infirm as not to be like to bear the voyage and change of air: these, with other impediments which God laid in my way, hindered me from putting my thoughts into execution.'

During the two years of his residence in London, previous to his final ejectment, Baxter preached in various places, as opportunities presented themselves.

He says: 'Being removed from my ancient flock in Worcestershire, and yet being uncertain whether I might return to them or not, I refused to take any other charge, but preached up and down London, for nothing, according as I was invited. When I had done thus above a year, I thought a fixed place was better, and so I joined with Dr. Bates, at St. Dunstan's in the West, in Fleet-street, and preached once a week, for which the people allowed me some maintenance. Before this time I scarcely ever preached a sermon in the city.

'The congregations being crowded was that which provoked envy to accuse me; and one day the crowd did drive me from my place. It fell out that, at Dunstan's church, in the midst of sermon, a little lime and dust, and perhaps a piece of a brick or two, fell down in the steeple or belfry, near the boys, which put the whole congregation into sudden melancholy, so that they thought that the steeple and church were falling; which put them all into so confused a haste to get away, that, indeed, the noise of the feet in the galleries sounded like the falling of the stones; so that the people crowded out of doors: the women left some of them a scarf, and some a shoe behind them, and some in the galleries cast themselves down upon those below, because they could not get down the stairs. I sat still down in the pulpit, seeing and pitying their vain distemper; and, as soon as I could be heard, I entreated their silence, and went on. The people were no sooner quieted, and got in again, and the auditory composed, but some that stood upon a wainscot bench, near the communion table, brake the bench with their weight, so that the noise renewed the fear again, and they were worse disordered than before; so that one old woman was heard, at the church door, asking forgiveness of God for not taking the first warning, and promising, if God would deliver her this once, she would take heed of coming thither again. When they were again quieted, I went on. But the church having before an ill name, as very old, and rotten, and dangerous, this put the parish upon a resolution to pull down all the roof and build it better; which they have done, with so great reparation of the walls and steeple, that it is now like a new church, and much more commodious for the hearers.

'Upon this reparation of Dunstan's church, I preached out my quarter at Bride's church in the other end of Fleet-street; where the common prayer being used by the curate before the sermon, I occasioned abundance to be at common prayer, who before avoided it. And yet accusations against me still continued.

'On the week days, Mr. Ashurst, with about twenty more citizens, desired me to preach a lecture in Milk-street, for which they allowed me £40 per annum, which I continued near a year, till we were all silenced. And at the same time, I preached once every Lord's Day at Blackfriars, where Mr. Gibbons, a judicious man, was minister. In Milk-street I took money, because it came not from the parishioners, but strangers, and so was no wrong to the minister, Mr. Vincent, a very holy, blameless man. But at Blackfriars I never took a penny, because it was the parishioners who called me, who would else be less able and ready to help their worthy pastor, who went to God, by a consumption, a little after he was silenced and put out. At these two churches I ended the course of my public ministry, unless God cause an undeserved resurrection.

'Shortly after our disputation at the Savoy, I went to Rickmansworth, in Hertfordshire, and preached there but once, upon Matthew 22:12, "And he was speechless"; where I spake not a word that was any nearer kin to sedition, or that had any greater tendency to provoke them, than by showing "that wicked men, and the refusers of grace, however they may now have many things to say to excuse their sins, will at last be speechless, and dare not stand to their wickedness before God." Yet did the Bishop of Worcester tell me, when he silenced me, that the Bishop of London had showed him letters from one of the hearers, assuring him that I preached seditiously; so little security was any man's innocency, who displeased the bishops, to his reputation with that party, which had but one auditor that desired to get favour by accusing him. So that a multitude of such experiences made me perceive, when I was silenced, that there was some mercy in it, in the midst of judgment; for I should scarce have preached a sermon, or put up a prayer to God, which one or other, through malice or hope of favour, would not have been tempted to accuse as guilty of some heinous crime. And, as Seneca saith, "He that hath an ulcer crieth Oh! if he do but think you touch him."

'Shortly after my return to London, I went into Worcestershire, to try whether it were possible to have any honest terms from the reading vicar there, that I might preach to my former flock; but when I had preached twice or thrice, he denied me liberty to preach any more. I offered him to take my lecture, which he was bound to allow me, under a bond of £500, but he refused it. I next offered him to be his curate, and he refused it. And, lastly, I desired leave but once to administer the sacrament to the people, and preach my farewell sermon to them, but he would not consent. At last I understood that he was directed by his superiors to do what he did. But Mr. Baldwin, an able preacher whom I left there, was yet permitted.

'At that time, my aged father lying in great pain of the stone and strangury, I went to visit him, twenty miles further; and while I was there, Mr. Baldwin came to me, and told me that he also was forbidden to preach. We returned both to Kidderminster.

'Having parted with my dear flock, I need not say with mutual sense and tears, I left Mr. Baldwin to live privately among them, and oversee them in my stead, and visit them from house to house; advising them, notwithstanding all the injuries they had received, and all the failings of the ministers that preached to them, and the defects of the present way of worship, that yet they should keep to public assemblies, and make use of such helps as might be had in public, together with their private help.'

The great crisis, which was foreseen by many, had now arrived. The parliamentary attempt to promote ecclesiastical peace, by the Act of Uniformity, ended in the ejectment of two thousand of the best and holiest ministers in the land from their livings and labours. Baxter determined on not taking the oath, and hence relinquished public preaching as soon as the act was passed, and before it came into operation. His reason for so doing, he states to be, that as his example was looked to by many throughout the country, it might be known that he could not conform.

Marriage

In the earlier period of his ministry, Baxter had resolved not to enter into the married state, that he might pursue his pastoral and ministerial labours with less anxiety and interruption. After his ejectment, however, having no public charge, and seeing little prospect of ever being able to resume his ministerial engagements, he deemed himself at liberty, and that it would conduce his comfort, to be united in the bonds of matrimony. He married Miss Charlton, a lady who, though much younger than himself, proved to be in every respect a suitable partner for this eminent saint.

His marriage excited much curiosity and remark throughout the kingdom; and 'I think,' he observes, 'the king's marriage was scarce more talked of than mine.' He and his wife lived a very unsettled life; being obliged, on account of persecutions, frequently to remove from one place of residence to another.

Moves to the country to live

'Having lived three years and more in London, since I left Kidderminster, but only three-quarters of a year since my marriage, and finding it neither agree with my health or studies, the one being brought very low, and the other interrupted, and all public service being at an end, I betook myself to live in the country, at Acton, that I might set myself to writing, and do what service I could for posterity, and live, as much as I possibly could, out of the world. Thither I came 1663, July 14, where I followed my studies privately in quietness, and went every Lord's Day to the public assembly, when there was any preaching or catechising, and spent the rest of the day with my family, and a few poor neighbours that came in; spending now and then a day in London. And the next year, 1664, I had the company of divers godly faithful friends that tabled with me in summer, with whom I solaced myself with much content.

'On March 26, being the Lord's Day, 1665, as I was preaching in a private house, where we received the Lord's Supper, a bullet came in at the window among us, and passed by me, and narrowly missed the head of a sister-in-law of mine that was there, and hurt none of us; and we could never discover whence it came.

'In June following, an ancient gentlewoman, with her sons and daughter, came four miles, in her coach, to hear me preach in my family, as out of special respect to me. It fell out that, contrary to our custom, we let her knock long at the door, and did not open it; and so a second time, when she had gone away and came again; and the third time she came when we had ended. She was so earnest to know when she might come again to hear me, that I appointed her a time. But, before she came, I had secret intelligence, from one that was nigh her, that she came with a heart exceeding full of malice, resolving, if possible, to do me what mischief she could by accusation; and so that danger was avoided.'

The Great Plague
The plague of London now burst forth with tremendous fury, on which Baxter thus remarks:

'And now, after all the breaches on the churches, the ejection of the ministers, and impenitency under all, wars, and plague, and danger of famine began all at once on us. War with the Hollanders, which yet continueth; and the driest winter, and spring, and summer that ever man alive knew, or our forefathers mention of late ages; so that the grounds were burnt like the highways where the cattle should have fed! The meadow grounds, where I lived, bare but four loads of hay, which before bare forty. The plague hath seized on the most famous and most excellent city of Christendom; and, at this time, eight thousand and near three hundred die of all diseases in a week. It hath scattered and consumed the inhabitants, multitudes being dead and fled. The calamities and cries of the diseased and impoverished are not to be conceived by those that are absent from them! Every man is a terror to his neighbour and himself; for God, for our sins, is a terror to us all. Oh! how is London, the place which God hath honoured with his gospel above all the places of the earth, laid low in horrors, and wasted almost to desolation, by the wrath of God, whom England hath contemned; and a God-hating generation are consumed in their sins, and the righteous are also taken away, as from greater evil yet to come.

'The number that died in London, besides all the rest of the land, was about a hundred thousand, reckoning the Quakers, and others that were never put in the bills of morality, with those that were in the bills. The richer sort removing out of the city, the greatest blow fell on the poor. At the first, so few of the most religious sort were taken away, that, according to the mode of too many such, they began to be puffed up, and boast of the great difference which God did make; but quickly after, they all fell alike. Yet not many pious ministers were taken away: I remember but three, who were all of my own acquaintance.

'It is scarce possible for people, that live in a time of health and security, to apprehend the dreadfulness of that pestilence! How fearful people were, thirty or forty, if not a hundred miles from London, of anything that they bought from any mercer's or draper's shop! or of any goods that were brought to them! or of any person that came to their houses! How they would shut their doors against their friends! and, if a man passed over the fields, how one would avoid another, as we did in the time of wars; and how every man was a terror to another! Oh, how sinfully unthankful are we for our quiet societies, habitations, and health!'

Many of the ejected ministers seized the opportunity of preaching in the neglected or deserted pulpits, and in the public places of resort, to the terror-stricken inhabitants of London; and blessed results followed. 'Those heard them one day often, that were sick the next, and quickly died. The face of death did so awaken both the preachers and the hearers, that preachers exceeded themselves in lively, fervent preaching, and the people crowded constantly to hear them; and all was done with such great seriousness, as that, through the blessing of God, abundance were converted from their carelessness, inpenitency, and youthful lusts and vanities; and religion took that hold on the people's hearts, as could never afterward be loosed.'

When the plague reached Acton, in July, Mr. Baxter retired from the scene to Hampden, in Bucks, where he continued with his friend, Mr. Hampden, till the following March. The plague, he says, 'being ceased on March 1 following, I returned home, and found the churchyard like a ploughed field with graves, and many of my neighbours dead; but my house, near the churchyard, uninfected, and that part of my family which I left there, all safe, through the great mercy of God, my merciful Protector.'

Scarcely had the plague ceased its ravages on the lives, before the great fire commenced its destructive career in London. Churches in great abundance were destroyed in the general conflagration. The zealous, though silenced watchmen, ventured amid the ashes of a ruined city, to urge the inhabitants to flee from the 'wrath to come', and to seek, in their impoverished condition, 'the unsearchable riches of Christ'.

The distress occasioned by these calamities was great. 'Many thousands were cast into utter want and beggary, and many thousands of the formerly rich were disabled from relieving them.' To the friends of Christ in London, the silenced ministers in the country had been accustomed to look for assistance in their distresses. By these providences their resources were in a measure dried up. But, though enduring dreadful privations, few, if any, were suffered to perish through want. Baxter says:

'Whilst I was living at Acton, as long as the act against conventicles was in force, though I preached to my family, few came to hear me of the town, partly because they thought it would endanger me, and partly for fear of suffering themselves; but especially because they were an ignorant poor people, and had no appetite for such things. But when the act was expired, there came so many that I wanted room; and when once they had come and heard, they afterwards came constantly. Insomuch that in a little time there was a great number of them that seemed very seriously affected with the things they heard, and almost all the town and parish, besides abundance from Brentford and the neighbouring parishes, came; and I know not of three in the parish that were adversaries to us or our endeavours, or wished us ill.'

He attended the services of the parish church, and between the interval of service he preached in his own house, opposite to the church, to as many as chose to come.

This gave umbrage to the minister of the parish. 'It pleased the parson,' says Baxter, 'that I came to church, and brought others with me; but he was not able to bear the sight of people's crowding into my house, though they heard him also; so that, though he spake me fair, and we lived in seeming love and peace while he was there, yet he could not long endure it. And when I had brought the people to church to hear him, he would fall upon them with groundless reproaches, as if he had done it purposely to drive them away; and yet thought that my preaching to them, because it was in a house, did all the mischief, though he never accused me of anything that I spake. For I preached nothing but Christianity and submission to our superiors; faith, repentance, hope, love, humility, self-denial, meekness, patience, and obedience.'

During his residence at Acton, Baxter became acquainted with Lord Chief Justice Hale, who occupied the house adjoining his own. With his simplicity, integrity, piety, and learning, he was delighted and charmed. He denominates him 'the pillar of justice, the refuge of the subject who feared oppression, and one of the greatest honours of his majesty's government'. His lordship, too, appears to have been equally interested in the character of his neighbour. His avowed esteem and respect for the despised nonconformist was a means of encouraging and strengthening the hands of Baxter. 'When the people crowded in and out of my house to hear, he openly showed me such great respect before them at the door, and never spake a word against it, as was no small encouragement to the common people to go on; though the other sort muttered that a judge should seem so far to countenance that which they took to be against the law.'

5

Persecution for the Faith

At length Baxter's preaching at Acton could no longer be connived at. Information was laid against him, and a warrant was issued for his apprehension. He was taken before two justices of the peace. 'When I came,' he writes, 'they shut out all persons from the room, and would not give leave for any one person, no, not their own clerk or servant, or the constable, to hear a word that was said between us. Then they told me that I was convicted of keeping conventicles contrary to law, and so they would tender me the Oxford oath. I desired my accusers might come face to face, and that I might see and speak with the witnesses who testified that I kept conventicles contrary to the law, which I denied, as far as I understood law; but they would not grant it. I pressed that I might speak in the hearing of some witnesses, and not in secret; for I supposed that they were my judges, and that their presence and business made the place a place of judicature, where none should be excluded, or at least some should be admitted. But I could not prevail.

'Had I resolved on silence, they were resolved to proceed; and I thought a Christian should rather submit to violence, and give place to injuries, than stand upon his right, when it will give others occasion to account him obstinate. I asked him whether I might freely speak for myself, and they said yea; but, when I began to speak, still interrupted me, and put me by. But, with much importunity,

I got them once to hear me, while I told them why I took not
my meeting to be contrary to law, and why the Oxford act
concerned me not, and they had no power to put that oath
on me by that act; but all the answer I could get was "that
they were satisfied of what they did". And when, among
other reasonings against their course, I told them, though
Christ's ministers had, in many ages, been men esteemed,
and used as we now are, and their afflicters had insulted
over them, the providence of God had still so ordered it,
that the names and memory of their silencers and afflicters
have been left to posterity for a reproach, insomuch that I
wondered that those who fear not God, and care not for
their own or the people's souls, should yet be so careless of
their fame, when honour seemeth so great a matter with them.
To which Ross answered, that he desired no greater honour
to his name, than that it should be remembered of him that
he did this against me, and such as I, which he was doing.'

The result of this interview was, that Baxter was fully
committed, for six months, to the New Prison, Clerkenwell.
He begged that his liberty might be granted till the following
Monday, but, as he would not promise not to preach on the
intervening Lord's Day, his request was denied.

The inhabitants of Acton were grieved at the loss of
their neighbour, and the more so, as the incumbent of the
parish was the means of his imprisonment. 'The whole
town of Acton were greatly exasperated against the Dean,
when I was going to prison, insomuch as ever since they
abhorred him as a selfish persecutor. Nor could he devise
to do more to hinder the success of his (seldom) preaching
there. But it was his own choice: "Let them hate me, so
they fear me." And so I finally left that place, being grieved
most that Satan had prevailed to stop the poor people in

such hopeful beginnings of a common reformation, and that I was to be deprived of the exceeding grateful neighbourhood of the Lord Chief Justice Hale, who could scarce refrain tears when he did but hear of the first warrant for my appearance.

'My imprisonment was, at present, no great suffering to me, for I had an honest jailer, who showed me all the kindness he could. I had a large room, and the liberty of walking in a fair garden; and my wife was never so cheerful a companion to me as in prison, and was very much against me seeking to be released; and she had brought so many necessaries, that we kept house as contendedly and as comfortably as at home, though in a narrower room; and I had the sight of more of my friends in a day than I had at home in half a year.'

Efforts were made by his friends to procure his release, which, in consequence of some informalities in his mittimus, were successful. His reflections on his imprisonment show the piety and submission of the venerable saint.

'Whilst I stayed in prison I saw somewhat to blame myself for, and somewhat to wonder at others for, and somewhat to advise my visitors about.

'I blamed myself that I was no more sensible of the spiritual part of my affliction; such as was the interruption of my work, and the poor people from whom I was removed, and the advantage Satan had got against them, and the loss of my own public liberty for worshipping in the assemblies of His servants.

'I marvelled at some who suffered no more than I, as Mr. Rutherford, when he was confined to Aberdeen, that their sufferings occasioned them such great joys as they express which surely was from the free grace of God, to encourage others by their examples, and not that their own impatience made them need it much more than at other times. For surely so small a suffering needeth not a quarter of the patience as many poor nonconforming ministers, and thousands of others, need, that are at liberty; whose own houses, through poverty, are made far worse to them than my prison was to me.

'To my visitors, I found reason to entreat my Acton neighbours, not to let their passion against their parson, on my account, hinder them from a due regard to his doctrine, nor from any of the duty which they owed him; and to blame some who aggravated my sufferings, and to tell them that I had no mind to fancy myself hurt before I felt it. I used, at home, to confine myself voluntarily almost as much. I had tenfold more public a life here, and converse with my friends, than I had at home. If I had been to take lodgings at London for six months, and had not known that this had been a prison, and had knocked at the door and asked for rooms, I should as soon have taken this which I was put into as most in town, save only for the interruption of my sleep. That it showeth great weakness to magnify a small suffering, and much worse to magnify ourselves and our own patience for bearing so small a thing; than which most poor men in England bear more every day.

'I found cause to desire my brethren, that, when they suffered, they would remember that the design of Satan was more against their souls than their bodies; and that it was not the least of his hopes to destroy their love, which was due to those by whom they suffered, and to dishonour superiors, and, by aggravating our suffering, to render them odious to the people. As also to make us take such a poor suffering as this for a sign of true grace, instead of faith, hope, love, mortification and a heavenly mind; and that the loss of one grain of love was worse than a long imprisonment. And that it much more concerned us to be sure that we deserved not suffering, than that we be delivered from it; and to see that we wronged not our superiors than that they wrong not us; seeing we are not near so much hurt by their severities as we are by our sins. Some told me that they hoped this would make me stand a little further from the prelates and their worship than I had done. To whom I answered that I wondered they should think that a prison should change my judgment. I rather thought now it was my duty to set a stricter watch upon my passions, lest they should pervert my judgment, and carry me into extremes in opposition to my afflicters. If passion made me lose my love or my religion, the loss would be my own. And truth did not change because I was in jail.'

His time was now chiefly occupied in writing and publishing various works on controversial and experimental divinity, and in making some attempts to procure a union between the Presbyterians and Independents. He frequently conversed and corresponded with Dr. John Owen on this subject. Owen requested Baxter to draw up a scheme of agreement. This scheme Owen attentively considered, but could not adopt, and concluded his correspondence with Baxter on this subject with observing, 'I am a well-wisher of these mathematics.' Baxter's attempts to unite all parties satisfied none. His method of uniting all would have compromised the principles of all. No efforts ever have been able to unite Episcopacy, Presbyterianism, and Independency, so as to form one common religious government and discipline. The principles on which each is founded are so diverse from those of the others, that union, without compromise, has not yet been effected. But the friends of each may 'agree to differ'; and, while each prefers his own communion, all may unite, without compromise, and in most perfect harmony, in various institutions now established to disseminate the knowledge of the truth, and promote the happiness of mankind. Many societies afford delightful opportunities for the union of all parties, and for the most abundant display of the charities of the gospel.

Baxter, with a few others of the nonconformists, defended the practice of occasional attendance and communion in the parish churches where the gospel was preached. It was, in consequence, currently reported, at this time, that he had actually conformed. He was offered preferment in Scotland by the king. A mitre, a professor's gown, or a surplice was presented to his choice. But he declined accepting his majesty's offer. His refusal is contained in his letter to the Earl of Lauderdale, through whom the offer was presented.

'My Lord,
'Being deeply sensible of your lordship's favours, and in special of your liberal offers for my entertainment in Scotland, I humbly return you my very hearty thanks. But these considerations forbid me to entertain any hopes or further thoughts of such a remove:

'1. The experience of my great weakness and decay of strength, and particularly of this last winter's pain, and how much worse I am in winter than in summer, doth fully persuade me that I shall live but a little while in Scotland, and that in a disabled, useless condition, rather keeping my bed than the pulpit.

'2. I am engaged in writing a book, which, if I could

hope to live to finish, is almost all the service that I expect
to do God and his church more in the world – a Latin
Methodus Theologiæ; and I can hardly hope to live so
long, it requiring near a year's labour more. Now, if I should
go spend that one half year, or year, which should finish
that work, in travel, and the trouble of such a removal, and
then leaving my intended work undone, it would disappoint
me of the ends of my life; for I live only for work, and
therefore should remove only for work, and not for wealth
and honour, if ever I remove.

'3. If I were there, all that I could hope for were liberty
to preach the gospel of salvation, and especially in some
university among young scholars. But I hear that you have
enough already for this work, that are like to do it better
than I can.

'4. I have a family, and in it a mother-in-law, of eighty
years of age, of honourable extraction and great worth,
whom I must not neglect, and who cannot travel. And it is
to such a one as I, so great a business to remove a family,
and all our goods and books, so far, as deterreth me to
think of it, having paid so dear for removals these eight years
as I have done, and being but yesterday settled in a house
which I have newly taken, and that with great trouble and
loss of time; and if I should find Scotland disagree with
me, which I fully conclude of, to remove all back again.

'All this concurreth to deprive me of this benefit of your
lordship's favour. But, my lord, there are other fruits of it,
which I am not altogether hopeless of receiving. When I
am commanded to pray for kings, and all in authority, I am
allowed the ambition of this preferment, which is all that
ever I aspired after, "to live a quiet and peaceable life, in
all godliness and honesty".

'I am weary of the noise of contentious revilers, and have often had thoughts to go into a foreign land, if I could find anywhere I might have a healthful air and quietness, that I might but live and die in peace. When I sit in a corner, and meddle with nobody, and hope the world will forget that I am alive, court, city, and country is still filled with clamours against me; and when a preacher wanteth preferment, his way is to preach or write a book against the nonconformists, and me by name. So that the press and pulpits of some utter bloody invectives against myself, as if my peace were inconsistent with the kingdom's happiness. And never did my eyes read such impudent untruths, in matter of fact, as these writings contain; and they cry out for answers and reasons of my nonconformity, while they know the law forbiddeth me to answer them unlicensed. I expect not that any favour or justice of my superiors should cure any of this. But,

'1. If I might but be heard speak for myself, before I be judged by them, and such things believed. For to contemn the judgment of my rulers, is to dishonour them.

'2. If I might live quietly to follow my private study, and might once again have the use of my books, which I have not seen these ten years, and pay for a room for their standing at Kidderminster, where they are eaten with worms and rats, having no security for my quiet abode in any place enough to encourage me to send for them. And if I might have the liberty that every beggar hath, to travel from town to town – I mean but to London, to oversee the press, when anything of mine is licensed for it. And,

'3. If I be sent to Newgate for preaching Christ's gospel, for I dare not sacrilegiously renounce my calling, to which I am consecrated; if I have the favour of a better prison, where I may but walk and write.

'These I should take as very great favours, and acknowledge your lordship my benefactor if you procure them. For I will not so much injure you as to desire, or my reason as to expect, any greater matters; no, not the benefit of the law. I think I broke no law in any of the preachings which I am accused of; and I most confidently think that no law imposeth on me the Oxford oath, any more than any conformable minister; and I am past doubting the present mittimus for my imprisonment is quite without law. But if the justices think otherwise now, or at any time, I know no remedy. I have yet a licence to preach publicly in London diocese under the Archbishop's own hand and seal, which is yet valid for occasional sermons, though not for lectures or cures; but I dare not use it. Would but the bishop, who, one would think, should not be against the preaching of the gospel, not recall my licence, I could preach occasional sermons, which would absolve my conscience from all obligations to private preaching. For it is not maintenance that I expect: I never received a farthing for my preaching, to my knowledge, since May 1, 1662. I thank God, I have food and raiment without being chargeable to any man, which is all that I desire, had I but leave to preach for nothing, and that only where there is a notorious necessity. I humbly crave your lordship's pardon for the tediousness, and again return you my very great thanks for your great favours, remaining,

'June 24, 1670.

'Richard Baxter.'

He says: 'On October 11, 1672, I fell into a dangerous fit of sickness, which God, in his wonted mercy, did in time so far remove, as to return me to some capacity of service.

'I had till now forborne, for several reasons, to seek a licence for preaching from the king, upon the Toleration. But when all others had taken theirs, and were settled in London, and other places, as they could get opportunity, I delayed no longer, but sent to seek one, on condition I might have it without the title of Independent, Presbyterian, or any other party, but only as a nonconformist. And before I sent, Sir Thomas Player, Chamberlain of London, had procured it me so, without my knowledge or endeavour. I sought none so long,

'1. Because I was unwilling to be or seem any cause of that way of liberty, if a better might have been had, and therefore would not meddle in it.

'2. I lived ten miles from London, and thought it not just to come and set up a congregation there till the ministers had fully settled theirs, who had borne the burden there in the times of the raging plague and fire and other calamities, lest I should draw away any of their auditors, and hinder their maintenance.

'3. I perceived that no one, that ever I heard of till mine, could get a licence, unless he would be entitled in it a Presbyterian, Independent, Anabaptist, or of some sect.

'The 19th of November, my baptism day, was the first day, after ten year's silence, that I preached in a tolerated public assembly, though not yet tolerated in any consecrated church, but only, against law, in my own house.

'Some merchants set up a Tuesday's lecture in London, to be kept by six ministers at Pinners' Hall, allowing them twenty shillings apiece each sermon, of whom they chose me to be one.'

'January 24, 1672-3, I began a Friday lecture at Mr.

Turner's church in New-street, near Fetterlane, with great convenience, and God's encouraging blessing; but I never took a penny of money for it of any one. And on the Lord's Days I had no congregation to preach to, but occasionally to any that desire me, being unwilling to set up a church and become the pastor of any, or take maintenance, in this distracted and unsettled way, unless further changes shall manifest it to be my duty. Nor did I ever yet give the sacrament to any one person, but to my old flock at Kidderminster.

'On February 20, I took my house in Bloomsbury, in London, and removed thither after Easter with my family; God having mercifully given me three years' great peace among quiet neighbours at Totteridge, and much more health or ease than I expected, and some opportunity to serve him.'

In this situation he continued for some time, employing his flying pen and his unwearied efforts to promote the peace of the church, and to instruct and bless mankind. In April 1674, he writes: 'God hath so much increased my languishing, and laid me so low, that I have reason to think that my time on earth will not be long. And oh, how good hath the will of God proved hitherto to me! And will it not be best at last? Experience causeth me to say to his praise, Great peace have they that love his law, and nothing shall offend them; and though my flesh and heart do fail, God is the rock of my heart and my portion for ever.

'At this time came out my book called *The Poor Man's Family Book*, which the remembrance of the great use of Mr. Dent's *Plain Man's Pathway to Heaven*, now laid by, occasioned me to write, for poor country families, who cannot buy or read many books.'

Anxiously bent on doing good, and encouraged by the reception and success his *Poor Man's Family Book* met with, he prepared several other works for the promotion and increase of family religion. He justly believed that domestic piety was of the utmost importance for the maintenance and progress of piety. To promote 'household religion' he employed all his energies while at Kidderminster. In his *Reformed Pastor*, he urges ministers seriously to consider the subject. He says:

'The life of religion, and the welfare and glory both of the church and state, depend much on family government and duty. If we suffer the neglect of this, we shall undo all. What are we like to do ourselves to the reforming of a congregation, if all the work be cast on us alone, and masters of families neglect that necessary duty of their own by which they are bound to help us? If any good be begun by the ministry in any soul, a careless, prayerless, worldly family is likely to stifle it, or very much hinder it; whereas, if you could but get the rulers of families to do their duty, to take up the work where you left it, and help it on, what abundance of good might be done! I beseech you, therefore, if you desire the reformation and welfare of your people, do all you can to promote family religion....

'You are not likely to see any general reformation till you procure family reformation. Some little religion there may be here and there; but while it is confined to single persons, and is not promoted in the family circle, it will not prosper, nor promise much future increase.'

He prosecuted his Master's work with unwearied zeal, though suffering great bodily affliction, and exposed to much vexatious and embarrassing opposition.

Preaches in London

'Taking it to be my duty to preach while toleration doth continue, I removed, the last spring, to London, where my diseases increasing this winter, a constant headache added to the rest, and continuing strong for about half a year, constrained me to cease my Friday's lecture, and an afternoon sermon on the Lord's Days in my house, to my grief; and to preach only one sermon a week at St. James's market-house, where some had hired an inconvenient place. But I had great encouragement to labour there:

'1. Because of notorious necessity of the people; for it was noted for the habitation of the most ignorant, atheistical, and popish about London, and the greatness of the parish of St. Martin's made it impossible for the tenth, perhaps the twentieth, person in the parish to hear in the parish church. And the next parishes, St. Gile's and Clements Danes, were almost in the like case; besides that, the parson of our own parish, St. Gile's, where I lived, preached not, having been about three years suspended by the bishop upon a particular quarrel. And to leave ten or twenty for one, untaught in the parish, while most of the city churches are also burnt down, and unbuilt, one would think, should not be justified by Christians.

'2. Because, beyond my expectation, the people generally proved exceeding willing, and attentive, and tractable, and gave me great hopes of much success.

'On July 5, 1674, at our meeting over St. James's market-house, God vouchsafed us a great deliverance. A main beam, before weakened by the weight of the people, so cracked, that three times they ran in terror out of the room, thinking it was falling; but, remembering the like at Dunstan's in the West, I reproved their fear as causeless.

But the next day, taking up the boards, we found that two rents in the beam were so great, that it was a wonder of Providence that the floor had not fallen, and the roof with it, to the destruction of multitudes. The Lord make us thankful!

'It pleased God to give me marvellous great encouragement in my preaching at St. James's. The crack having frightened away most of the richer sort, especially the women, most of the congregation were young men, of the most capable age, who heard with very great attention; and many that had not come to church for many years received so much and manifested so great a change, some papists and divers others, returning public thanks to God for their conversion, as made all my charge and trouble easy to me. Among all the popish, rude, and ignorant people who were inhabitants of those parts, we had scarcely any that opened their mouths against us, and that did not speak well of the preaching of the word against them; though, when I came first thither, the most knowing inhabitants assured me that some of the same persons wished my death. Among the ruder sort, a common reformation was notified in the place, in their conversation as well as in their judgments.

'The dangerous crack over the market-house at St. James's put many upon desiring that I had a larger, safer place for meeting. And though my own dulness, and great backwardness to troublesome business, made me very averse to so great an undertaking, judging that, it being in the face of the court, it would never be endured, yet the great and incessant importunity of many, out of a fervent desire of the good of souls, did constrain me to undertake it. And when it was almost finished in Oxenden-street, Mr. Henry Coventry, one of his majesty's principal secretaries, who had a house joining to it, and was a Member of Parliament, spake twice against it in the Parliament; but no one seconded him.

'And that we might do the more good, my wife urged the building of another meeting-place, in Bloomsbury for Mr. Read, to be furthered by my sometime helping him; the neighbourhood being very full of people, rich and poor, that could not come into the parish church, through the greatness of the parish, and Dr. Bourman, the parish parson, having not preached, prayed, read, or administered sacraments these three or four years.

'I was so long wearied with keeping my door shut against them that came to distrain[1] on my goods for preaching, that I was fain to go from my house, and to sell all my goods, and to hide my library first, and afterwards to sell it. So that if books had been my treasure, and I valued little more on earth, I had been now without a treasure. About twelve years I was driven a hundred miles from them; and when I had paid dear for the carriage, after two or three years I was forced to sell them. And the prelates, to hinder me from preaching, deprived me also of these private comforts. But God saw that they were my snare. We brought nothing into the world, and we must carry nothing out. The loss is very tolerable.

'I was the more willing to part with goods, books, and all, that I might have nothing to be distrained, and so go on to preach. And, accordingly, removing my dwelling to the new chapel which I had built, I purposed to venture there to preach, there being forty thousand persons in the parish, as is supposed, more than can hear in the parish church, who have no place to go to for God's public worship. So

---

1. Distrain: seize goods in default of payment.

that I set not up church against church, but preached to those that must else have none, being loth that London should turn atheist, or live worse than infidels. But when I had preached there but once, a resolution was taken to surprise me the next day, and send me for six months to the common jail, upon the act for the Oxford oath.

'Not knowing of this, it being the hottest part of the year, I agreed to go for a few weeks into the country, twenty miles off. But the night before I should go, I felt so ill, that I was fain to send to disappoint both the coach and my intended companion, Mr. Silvester. And when I was thus fully resolved to stay, it pleased God, after the ordinary coach hour, that three men, from three parts of the city, met at my house accidentally, just at the same time, almost to a minute, of whom if any one had not been there, I had not gone; namely the coachman again to urge me, Mr. Silvester, whom I had put off, and Dr. Coxe, who compelled me, and told me else he would carry me into the coach. It proved a special merciful providence of God; for, after one week of languishing and pain, I had nine weeks' greater ease than ever I expected in this world, and greater comfort in my work. For my good friend, Richard Berisford, Esq., clerk of the exchequer, whose importunity drew me to his house, spared for no cost, labour, or kindness, for my health or service.'

Baxter was now constantly harassed with informations, fines, and warrants of distress, but he bore them all with astonishing meekness and patience. He endeavoured to convince and convert the informers and officers, who, on several occasions, came to apprehend him. In some cases his exhortations were successful, if not to their actual conversion, at least to induce them to relinquish their persecuting practices.

A striking instance of his placable and forgiving disposition is given in the following extract.

'Keting, the informer, being commonly detested for prosecuting me, was cast into jail for debt, and wrote to me to endeavour his deliverance, which I did; and in his letters saith, "Sir, I assure you, I do verily believe that God hath bestowed all his affliction on me, because I was so vile a wretch as to trouble you. And I assure you I never did a thing in my life that hath so much troubled myself as that did. And, truly, I do not think of any that went that way to work, that ever God would favour him with his mercy. And, truly, without a great deal of mercy from God, I do not think that ever I shall thrive or prosper. And I hope you will be pleased to pray to God for me." '

Baxter considered that the 'vows of God were upon him', and that he must continue to preach wherever Divine providence opened a door for the purpose. His obligations to God he considered as superior to those by which he was bound to obey the ordinances of man; and therefore, though forbidden by law, and in despite of persecution, he continued to preach the gospel to his ignorant and perishing countrymen.

He says: 'Being driven from home, and having an old licence of the bishop's yet in force, by the countenance of that, and the great industry of Mr. Berisford, I had leave and invitation for ten Lord's Days to preach in the parish churches round about. The first parish that I preached in, after thirteen years' ejection and prohibition, was Rickmansworth, and, after that, at Sarratt, at King's Langley, at Chesham, at Chalfont, and at Amersham, and that often twice a day. Those heard that had not come to church for seven years; and two or three thousand heard, where scarcely a hundred were wont to come; and with so much attention and willingness, as gave me very great hopes that I never spake to them in vain. And thus soul and body had these special mercies.

'When I had been kept a whole year from preaching in the chapel which I built, on the 16th of April, 1676, I began in another, in a tempestuous time; for the necessity of the parish of St. Martin's, where about 60,000 souls have no church to go to, nor any public worship of God! How long, Lord?

'Being denied forcibly the use of the chapel which I had built, I was forced to let it stand empty, and pay thirty pounds per annum for the ground-rent myself, and glad to preach for nothing near it, at a chapel built by another, formerly in Swallow-street, because it was among the same poor people that had no preaching; the parish having 60,000 souls in it more than the church can hold.'

Interruptions and informations were so numerous at Swallow-street, that he was obliged to discontinue his labours there. 'It pleased God to take away, by torment of the stone, that excellent and faithful minister, Mr. Thomas Wadsworth, in Southwark; and just when I was thus kept out at Swallow-street, his flock invited me to Southwark, where, though I refused to be their pastor, I preached many months in peace, there being no justice willing to disturb us.

'When Dr. Lloyd became pastor of St. Martin's-in-the-Fields, I was encouraged by Dr. Tillotson to offer him my chapel in Oxenden-street for public worship, which he accepted to my great satisfaction, and now there is constant preaching there. Be it by conformists or nonconformists, I rejoice that Christ is preached to the people in that parish, whom ten or twenty such chapels cannot hold.'

His reputation, too, was assailed. He was charged with uttering falsehood, and with the crime of murder. He was able, however, successfully to refute the calumnies, and to confound his calumniators.

About this period, 1681, Baxter was called to endure a severe and trying providence, in the death of his wife. They had lived together for nineteen years. She had been his companion in tribulation, his comforter in sorrow. Animated by her piety and her influence, he had persevered in all his attempts to do good. But now, in the advance of life, in weakened health, in persecution, and in no distant prospect of imprisonment, he was left to pursue his journey alone. She died in the faith and hope of the gospel, and was buried in Christ Church on June 17, 1681.

He still pursued his studies and his occasional labours. 'Having been for retirement in the country, from July till August 14, 1682, returning in great weakness, I was able only to preach twice, of which the last was in my usual lecture in New Street, and it fell out to be August 24, just that day twenty years that I, and near two thousand more, had been by law forbidden to preach any more. I was sensible of God's wonderful mercy that had kept so many of us twenty years in so much liberty and peace, while so many severe laws were in force against us, and so great a number were round about us who lacked neither malice nor power to afflict us. And so I took, that day, my leave of the pulpit and public work, in a thankful congregation. And it is like, indeed, to be my last.'

Increased opposition

'But after this, when I had ceased preaching, I was, being newly risen from extremity of pain, suddenly surprised in my house by a poor violent informer, and many constables and officers, who rushed in and apprehended me, and served on me one warrant to seize on my person, for coming within five miles of a corporation; and five more warrants, to distrain for a hundred and ninety pounds for five sermons. They cast my servants into fears, and were about to take all my books and goods, and I contentedly went with them towards the justice to be sent to jail, and left my house to their will. But Dr. Thomas Coxe, meeting me, forced me in again to my couch and bed, and went to five justices and took his oath, without my knowledge, that I could not go to prison without danger of death. Upon that, the justices delayed a day, till they could speak with the king, and told him what the doctor had sworn; and the king consented that the present imprisonment should be forborne, that I might die at home. But they executed all their warrants on my books and goods, even the bed that I lay sick on, and sold them all; and some friends paid them as much money as they were prized at, which I repaid, and was fain to send them away.

'When I borrowed some necessaries I was never the quieter; for they threatened to come upon me again, and take all as mine, whosesoever it was, which they found in my possession. So that I had no remedy, but utterly to forsake my house, and goods, and all, and take secret lodgings distant in a stranger's house. But, having a long lease of my own house, which binds me to pay a greater rent than now it is worth, whenever I go I must pay that rent.

'The separation from my books would have been a

greater part of my small affliction, but that I found I was
near the end both of that work and life which needeth books,
and so I easily let go all. Naked came I into the world, and
naked must I go out.

'But I never wanted less what man can give, than when
men had taken all. My old friends, and strangers to me,
were so liberal that I was fain to restrain their bounty.
Their kindness was a surer and larger revenue to me than
my own.

'But God was pleased quickly to put me past all fear of
man, and all desire of avoiding suffering from them by
concealment, by laying on me more himself than man can
do. Their imprisonment, with tolerable health, would have
seemed a palace to me; and had they put me to death for
such a duty as they persecute me, it would have been a
joyful end of my calamity. But day and night I groan and
languish under God's just afflicting hand. As waves follow
waves in the tempestuous seas, so one pain and danger
followeth another in this sinful, miserable flesh. I die daily,
and yet remain alive. God in his great mercy, knowing my
dulness in health and ease, doth make it much easier to
repent, and hate my sin, and loathe myself, and contemn
the world, and submit to the sentence of death with
willingness, than otherwise it was ever like to have been.
Oh how little is it that wrathful enemies can do against us,
in comparison of what our sin and the justice of God can
do! And oh how little is it that the best and kindest of friends
can do for a pained body, or a guilty, sinful soul, in
comparison of one gracious look or work from God! Woe
be to him that hath no better help than man! and blessed is
he whose help and hope is in the Lord.

'While I continued night and day under constant pain,

and often strong, and under the sentence of approaching
death by an incurable disease, which age and great debility
yields to, I found great need of the constant exercise of
patience by obedient submission to God; and, writing a
small tractate of it for my own use, I saw reason to yield to
them that desired it might be public, there being especially
so common need of "obedient patience".

'Under my daily pains I was drawn to a work which I
had never the least thoughts of, and is like to be the last of
my life, to write a paraphrase on the New Testament. Mr.
John Humphrey having long importuned me to write a
paraphrase on the Epistle to the Romans, when I had done
that, the usefulness of it to myself drew me farther and
farther till I had done all. But having confessed my ignorance
of the Revelation, and yet loth wholly to omit it, I gave but
general notes, with the reasons of my uncertainty in the
greatest difficulties, which I know will fall under the sharp
censure of many. But truth is more valuable than such men's
praises. I fitted the whole, by plainness, to the use of
ordinary families.

'After many times' deliverance from the sentence of
death, on November 20, 1684, in the very entrance of the
seventieth year of my age, God was pleased so greatly to
increase my painful diseases, as to pass on me the sentence
of a painful death. But God turneth it to my good, and giveth
me a greater willingness to die, than I once thought I should
ever have attained. The Lord teach me more fully to love
his will, and rest therein, as much better than my own, that
often striveth against it.

'A little before this, while I lay in pain and languishing,
the justices of sessions sent warrants to apprehend me,
about a thousand more being in catalogue, to be all bound

to the good behaviour. I thought they would send me six months to prison for not taking the Oxford oath, and dwelling in London, and so I refused to open my chamber door to them, their warrant not being to break it open. But they set six officers at my study door, who watched all night, and kept me from my bed and food; so that the next day I yielded to them, who carried me, scarce able to stand, to their sessions, and bound me, in a four hundred pounds' bond, to the good behaviour.

'I desired to know what my crime was, and who were my accusers; but they told me it was for no fault, but to secure the government in evil times; and that they had a list of many suspected persons, who must do the like, as well as I. I desired to know for what I was numbered with the suspected, and by whose accusation, but they gave me good words, and would not tell me.

'I told them I would rather they would send me to jail, than put me to wrong others by being bound with me, in bonds that I was like to break to-morrow; for, if there did but five persons come in when I was praying, they would take it for a breach of the good behaviour. They told me not, if they came on other business, unexpectedly, and not to a set meeting; nor yet if we did nothing contrary to law, or the practice of the church. I told them, our innocency was not now any security to us. If two beggar women did but stand in the street and swear that I spake contrary to the law, though they heard me not, my bonds and liberty were at their will; for I myself, lying on my bed, heard Mr. I. R. preach in a chapel on the other side of my chamber, and yet one Sibil Dash, and Elizabeth Cappell, swore to the justices that it was another that preached; two miserable poor women that made a trade of it, and had thus sworn against very many worthy persons in Hackney, and elsewhere, on which their goods were seized on for mulcts or fines. But to all this I had no answer, but must give bond, when they knew that I was not likely to break the behaviour, unless by lying in bed in pain.

'But all this is so small a part of my suffering, in comparison of what I bear in my flesh, that I could scarce regard it; and it is small in comparison of what others suffer. Many excellent persons die in common jails: thousands are ruined. That holy, humble man, Mr. Rosewell, is now under a verdict for death as a traitor for preaching some words, on the witness and oath of Hilton's wife, and one or two more women, whose husband liveth professedly on the trade, for which he claimeth many hundred or thousand pounds. And not only the man professeth, but many of his hearers witness, that no such words were spoken, nor any that beseemed not a loyal, prudent man.

'December 11, I was forced, in all my pain and weakness, to be carried to the sessions-house, or else my bond of four hundred pounds would have been judged forfeited. And the more moderate justices, that promised my discharge, would none of them be there, but left the work to Sir William Smith, and the rest who openly declared that they had nothing against me, and took me for innocent, but yet I must continue bound, lest others should expect to be discharged also, which I openly refused. But my sureties would be bound, lest I should die in jail, against my declared will, and so I must continue.

'January 17, I was forced again to be carried to the sessions, and, after divers days' good words, which put me in expectation of freedom, when I was gone, one justice, Sir-Deerham, said that it is like that these persons

solicited so for my liberty that they might come to hear me
in conventicles; and on that they bound me again, in a four
hundred pounds bond, for above a quarter of a year, and so
it is like it will be till I die, or worse; though no one ever
accused me for any conventicle or preaching, since they
took all my books and goods above two years ago, and I,
for the most part, keep my bed.'

6

Trial for Sedition

His greatest trial was now hastening. His *Paraphrase on the New Testament* gave great offence in certain quarters, and was made the ground of a trial for sedition.

The following account of this extraordinary trial and its issue are given by Calamy, and in a letter from a person who was present on the occasion. Baxter's biographer has included the information from both.

'On the 28th of February, Baxter was committed to the King's Bench prison, by warrant of Lord Chief Justice Jefferies, for his *Paraphrase on the New Testament*, which had been printed a little before, and which was described as a scandalous and seditious book against the government. On his commitment by the Chief Justice's warrant, he applied for a habeas corpus, and having obtained it, he absconded into the country to avoid imprisonment, till the term approached. He was induced to do this from the constant pain he endured, and an apprehension that he could not bear the confinement of a prison.

'On the 6th of May, which was the first day of the term, he appeared in Westminster Hall, and an information was then drawn up against him. On the 14th of May, he pleaded not guilty to the information. On the 18th of the same month, being much indisposed, it was moved that he might have further time given him before his trial, but this was denied him. He moved for it by his counsel; but Jefferies cried out in a passion, "I will not give him a minute's time more, to save his life. We have had to do," said he, "with other sorts of persons, but now we have a saint to deal with; and I know how to deal with saints as well as sinners. Yonder," said he, "stands Oates in the pillory," (as he actually did at that very time in the New Palace Yard,) "and he says he suffers for the truth, and so says Baxter; but if Baxter did but stand on the other side of the pillory with him, I would say, two of the greatest rogues and rascals in the kingdom stood there."

'On May 30, in the afternoon, Baxter was brought to trial before the Lord Chief Justice at Guildhall. Sir Henry Ashurst, who would not forsake his own and his father's friend, stood by him all the while. Baxter came first into court, and, with all the marks of sincerity and composure, waited for the coming of the Lord Chief Justice, who appeared quickly after, with great indignation in his face.

' "When I saw," says an eye-witness, "the meek man stand before the flaming eyes and fierce looks of this bigot, I thought of Paul standing before Nero. The barbarous usage which he received drew plenty of tears from my eyes, as well as from others of the auditors and spectators: yet I could not but smile sometimes, when I saw my lord imitate our modern pulpit drollery, which some one saith any man engaged in such a design would not lose for a world. He drove on furiously, like Hannibal over the Alps, with fire and vinegar, pouring all the contempt and scorn upon Baxter, as if he had been a link-boy or knave; which made the people who could not come near enough to hear the indictment or Mr. Baxter's plea, cry out, 'Surely, this Baxter had burned the city or the temple of Delphos.' But others said, it was not the custom, now-a-days, to receive ill, except for doing well; and therefore this must needs be some good man that my lord so rails at."

'Jefferies no sooner sat down than a short cause was called and tried; after which the clerk began to read the title of another cause. "You blockhead, you," said Jefferies, "the next cause is between Richard Baxter and the king:" upon which Baxter's cause was called.

'On the jury being sworn, Baxter objected to them, as incompetent to his trial, owing to its peculiar nature. The jury being tradesmen, and not scholars, he alleged they were incapable of pronouncing whether his "Paraphrase" was, or was not, according to the original text. He therefore prayed that he might have a jury of learned men, though the one-half of them should be papists. This objection, as might have been expected, was overruled by the court.

'The king's counsel opened the information at large, with its aggravations. Mr. Pollexfen, Mr. Wallop, Mr. Williams, Mr. Rotherman, Mr. Atwood and Mr. Phipps were Baxter's counsel, and had been feed by Sir Henry Ashurst.

'Pollexfen then rose and addressed the court and the jury. He stated that he was counsel for the prisoner, and felt that he had a very unusual plea to manage. He had been obliged, he said, by the nature of the cause to consult all our learned commentators, many of whom, learned, pious, and belonging to the church of England too, concurred with Mr. Baxter in his paraphrase of those passages of Scripture which were objected to in the indictment, and by whose help he would be enabled to manage his client's cause. "I shall begin," said he, "with Dr. Hammond; and, gentlemen, though Mr. Baxter made an objection against you, as not fit judges of Greek, which has been overruled, I hope you understand English, common sense, and can read." To which the foreman of the jury made a profound bow, and said, "Yes, sir."

'On this his lordship burst upon Pollexfen like a fury and told him he should not sit there to hear him preach.

' "No, my lord," said Mr. Pollexfen, "I am counsel for Mr. Baxter, and shall offer nothing but what is *ad rem* [to the point]."

' "Why, this is not," said Jefferies, "that you cant to the jury beforehand."

' "I beg your lordship's pardon," said the counsel, "and shall then proceed to business."

' "Come then," said Jefferies, "what do you say to this count? Read it, clerk:" referring to the paraphrase on Mark 12:38-40. "Is he not, now, an old knave, to interpret this as belonging to liturgies?"

' "So do others," replied Pollexfen, "of the church of England, who would be loth so to wrong the cause of liturgies as to make them a novel invention, or not to be able to date them as early as the scribes and Pharisees."

' "No, no, Mr. Pollexfen," said the judge: "they were long-winded, extempore prayers, such as they used to say when they appropriated God to themselves: 'Lord, we are thy people, thy peculiar people, thy dear people.' " And then he snorted, and squeaked through his nose, and clenched his hands, and lifted up his eyes mimicking their manner, and running on furiously, as he said they used to pray.

'But old Pollexfen gave him a bite now and then, though he could hardly get in a word. "Why, my lord," said he, "some will think it is a hard measure to stop these men's mouths, and not let them speak through their noses."

' "Pollexfen," said Jefferies, "I know you well; I will set a mark upon you: you are the patron of the faction. This is an old rogue, who has poisoned the world with his Kidderminster doctrine. Don't we know how he preached formerly, 'Curse ye Meroz; curse them bitterly that come not to the help of the Lord, to the help of the Lord against the mighty'? He encouraged all the women and maids to bring their bodkins and thimbles to carry on their war against the king of ever blessed memory. An old schismatical knave, a hypocritical villain."

' "I beseech your lordship," said Pollexfen, "suffer me a word for my client. It is well known to all intelligent men of age in this nation, that these things do not apply to the character of Mr. Baxter, who wished as well to the king and royal family as Mr. Love, who lost his head for endeavouring to bring in the son long before he was restored. And, my lord, Mr. Baxter's loyal and peaceable spirit King Charles would have rewarded with a bishopric, when he came in, if he would have conformed."

' "Ay, ay," said the judge, "we know that; but what ailed the old blockhead, the unthankful villain, that he would not conform? Was he wiser or better than other men? He hath been, ever since, the spring of the faction. I am sure he hath poisoned the world with his linsey-woolsey doctrine." Here his rage increased to an amazing degree. He called Baxter a conceited, stubborn, fanatical dog. "Hang him," said he; "this one old fellow hath cast more reproach upon the constitution and discipline of our church than will be wiped off these hundred years; but I'll handle him for it: for (with an oath) he deserves to be whipped through the city."

' "My lord," said Pollexfen, "I am sure these things are

not *ad rem*. Some persons think, my lord, it is very hard that these men should be forced against their consciences from the church. But that is not my business, my lord. I am not to justify their nonconformity, or give here the reasons of their scruples to accept beneficial places, but rather to suffer anything. I know not, my lord, what reasons sway other men's consciences; my business is to plead for my client, and to answer the charge of dangerous sedition, which is alleged to be contained in his *Paraphrase of the New Testament*."

'Mr. Wallop said, that he conceived, the matter depending being a point of doctrine, it ought to be referred to the bishop, his ordinary; but if not, he humbly conceived the doctrine was innocent and justifiable, setting aside the inuendos, for which there was no colour, there being no antecedent to refer them to (i.e., no bishop or clergy of the church of England named); he said the book accused, i.e., the *Comment on the New Testament*, contained many eternal truths: but they who drew the information were the libellers, in applying to the prelates of the church of England those severe things which were written concerning some prelates who deserved the characters which he gave. "My lord," said he, "I humbly conceived the bishops Mr. Baxter speaks of, as your lordship, if you have read church history, must confess, were the plagues of the church and of the world."

' "Mr. Wallop," said the Lord Chief Justice, "I observe you are in all these dirty causes: and were it not for you gentlemen of the long robe, who should have more wit and honesty than to support and hold up these factious knaves by the chin, we should not be at the pass we are."

' "My lord," replied Wallop, '" humbly conceive that

the passages accused are natural deductions from the text."

' "You humbly conceive," said Jefferies, "and I humbly conceive. Swear him, swear him."

' "My lord," said he, "under favour, I am counsel for the defendant, and if I understand either Latin or English, the information now brought against Mr. Baxter, upon such a slight ground, is a greater reflection upon the church of England than anything contained in the book he is accused for."

' "Sometimes you humbly conceive, and sometimes you are very positive," said Jefferies; "you talk of your skill in church history, and of your understanding Latin and English; I think I understand something of them as well as you; but, in short, must tell you, that if you do not understand your duty better, I shall teach it you." Upon which Mr. Wallop sat down.

'Mr. Rotherham urged "that if Mr. Baxter's book had sharp reflection upon the church of Rome by name, but spake well of the prelates of the church of England, it was to be presumed that the sharp reflections were intended only against the prelates of the church of Rome."

'The Lord Chief Justice said, "Baxter was an enemy to the name and thing, the office and persons, of bishops."

'Rotherham added "that Baxter frequently attended divine service, went to the sacrament, and persuaded others to do so too, as was certainly and publicly known; and had, in the very book so charged, spoken very moderately and honourably of the bishops of the church of England."

'Baxter added, "My lord, I have been so moderate with respect to the church of England, that I have incurred the censure of many of the dissenters upon that account."

' "Baxter for bishops!" exclaimed Jefferies, "that is a

merry conceit indeed: turn to it, turn to it."

'Upon this, Rotherham turned to a place where it is said, "that great respect is due to those truly called to be bishops among us;" or to that purpose.

' "Ay," said Jefferies, "this is your Presbyterian cant; truly called to be bishops: that is himself, and such rascals, called to be bishops of Kidderminster, and other such places. Bishops set apart by such factious, snivelling Presbyterians as himself: a Kidderminster bishop he means. According to the saying of a late learned author: And every parish shall maintain, a tithe-pig metropolitan."

'Baxter beginning to speak again, Jefferies reviled him. "Richard Baxter, dost thou think we'll hear thee poison the court? Richard, thou art an old fellow, an old knave; thou hast written books enough to load a cart, every one as full of sedition, I might say treason, as an egg is full of meat. Hadst thou been whipped out of thy writing trade forty years ago, it had been happy. Thou pretendest to be a preacher of the gospel of peace, and thou hast one foot in the grave: it is time for thee to begin to think what account thou intendest to give. But leave thee to thyself, and I see thou'lt go on as thou hast begun; but, by the grace of God, I'll look after thee. I know thou hast a mighty party, and I see a great many of the brotherhood in corners, waiting to see what will become of their mighty don, and a doctor of the party (looking to Dr. Bates) at your elbow; but, by the grace of Almighty God, I'll crush you all. Come, what do you say for yourself, you old knave? Come, speak up! What doth he say? I am not afraid of you, for all the snivelling calves you have got about you:" alluding to some persons who were in tears about Mr. Baxter.

' "Your lord-ship need not," said the holy man, "for I'll

not hurt you. But these things will surely be understood one day; what fools one sort of Protestants are made, to persecute the other." And, lifting up his eyes to heaven, said, "I am not concerned to answer such stuff; but am ready to produce my writings for the confutation of all this; and my life and conversation are known to many in this nation."

'Mr. Rotherham sitting down, Mr. Atwood began to show that not one of the passages mentioned in the information ought to be strained to the sense which was put upon them by the innuendos; they being more natural when taken in a milder sense: nor could any one of them be applied to the prelates of the church of England, without a forced construction. To prove this, he would have read some of the text: but Jefferies cried out, "You shan't draw me into a conventicle with your annotations, nor your snivelling parson neither."

' "My lord," said Mr. Atwood, "that I may use the best authority, permit me to repeat your lordship's own words in that case."

' "No, you shan't," said he, "you need not speak, for you are an author already; though you speak and write impertinently."

'Atwood replied, "I can't help that, my lord, if my talent be not better; but it is my duty to do my best for my client."

'Jefferies then went on inveighing against what Atwood had published; and Atwood justified it as in defence of the English constitution, declaring that he never disowned anything that he had written. Jefferies, several times, ordered him to sit down; but he still went on. "My lord," said he, "I have matter of law to urge for my client." He then proceeded to cite several cases wherein it had been adjudged that words ought to be taken in the milder sense, and not to be strained by innuendos.

' "Well," said Jefferies, when he had done, "you have had your say."

'Mr. Williams and Mr. Phipps said nothing, for they saw it was to no purpose. At last, Baxter himself said, "My lord, I think I can clearly answer all that is laid to my charge, and shall do it briefly. The sum is contained in these few papers, to which I shall add a little by testimony." But he would not hear a word.

'At length, the Chief Justice summed up the matter in a long and fulsome harangue. "It was notoriously known," he said, "there had been a design to ruin the king and the nation. The old game had been renewed; and this person had been the main incendiary. He is as modest now as can be; but time was, when no man was so ready at, 'Bind your kings in chains, and your nobles in fetters of irons;' and, 'To your tents, O Israel.' Gentlemen, (with an oath,) don't let us be gulled twice in an age." And when he concluded, he told the jury "that if they in their consciences believed he meant the bishops and clergy of the church of England, in the passages which the information referred to, and he could mean nothing else, they must find him guilty. If not, they must find him not guilty."

'When he had done, Baxter said to him, "Does your lordship think any jury will pretend to pass a verdict upon me upon such a trial?"

' "I'll warrant you, Mr. Baxter," said he, "don't you trouble yourself about that."

'The jury immediately laid their heads together at the bar, and found him guilty. As he was going from the bar, Baxter told the Lord Chief Justice, who had so loaded him

with reproaches, and still continued them, that a predecessor
of his had other thoughts of him; upon which he replied,
"that there was not an honest man in England but what took
him for a great knave."

'Baxter had subpœnaed several clergymen, who
appeared in court, but were of no use to him, through the
violence of the Chief Justice. The trial being over, Sir Henry
Ashurst led him through the crowd, and conveyed him away
in his coach.'

This is a faithful portrait of Jefferies, who furnished
Bunyan with the features of his Chief Justice, the Lord
Hategood. Can we be insensible to the mercies we enjoy
in the very different administration of justice in our own
times?

On the 29th of June, Baxter had judgment given against
him. He was fined five hundred marks, condemned to lie
in prison till he paid it, and bound to his good behaviour
for seven years. It is said that Jefferies proposed a corporal
punishment, namely, whipping through the city; but his
brethren would not accede to it. In consequence of which,
the fine and imprisonment were agreed to.

Baxter being unable to pay the fine, and aware that,
though he did, he might soon be prosecuted again, on some
equally unjust pretence, went to prison. Here he was visited
by his friends, and even by some of the respectable clergy
of the church, who sympathised with his sufferings, and
deplored the injustice he received. He continued in his
imprisonment nearly two years; during which he enjoyed
more quietness than he had done for many years before.

An imprisonment of two years would have been found
very trying and irksome to most men. To Baxter, however,
it does not appear to have proved so painful, though he had

now lost his beloved wife, who had frequently before been his companion in solitude and suffering. His friends do not appear to have neglected or forgotten him. The following extract of a letter, from the well-known Matthew Henry, presents a pleasing view of the manner in which he endured bonds for Christ's sake. It is addressed to his father, and dated the 17th of November, 1685, when Baxter had been several months confined. Mr. Williams justly remarks: 'It is one of those pictures of days which are past, which, if rightly viewed, may produce lasting and beneficial effects; emotions of sacred sorrow for the iniquity of persecution; and animating praise, that the demon in these happy days of tranquillity is restrained, though not destroyed.'

'I went into Southwark, to Mr. Baxter. I was to wait upon him once before, and then he was busy. I found him in pretty comfortable circumstances, though a prisoner, in a private house near the prison, attended by his own man and maid. My good friend, Mr. S[amuel] L[awrence]. went with me. He is in as good health as one can expect; and, methinks, looks better, and speaks heartier, than when I saw him last. The token you sent, he would by no means be persuaded to accept, and was almost angry when I pressed it, from one outed as well as himself. He said he did not use to receive; and I understand since, his need is not great.

'We sat with him about an hour. I was very glad to find that he had so much approved of my present circumstances. He said he knew not why young men might not improve as well as by travelling abroad. He inquired for his Shropshire friends, and observed, that of those gentlemen who were with him at Wem, he hears of none whose sons tread in their father's steps but Colonel Hunt's. He inquired about Mr. Macworth's and Mr. Lloyd of Aston's children.

He gave us some good counsel to prepare for trials; and said the best preparation for them was a life of faith and a constant course of self-denial. He thought it harder constantly to deny temptations to sensual lusts and pleasures, than to resist one single temptation to deny Christ for fear of suffering: the former requiring such constant watchfulness; however, after the former, the latter will be the easier. He said, we who are young are apt to count upon great things, but we must not look for them; and much more to this purpose. He said he thought dying by sickness usually much more painful and dreadful than dying a violent death; especially considering the extraordinary supports which those have who suffer for righteousness' sake.'

7

Closing Days

Various efforts were made by his friends to have his fine remitted, which, after considerable delay, was accomplished.

On the 24th of November, 1686, Sir Samuel Astrey sent his warrant to the keeper of the King's Bench prison, to discharge Baxter. He gave sureties, however, for his good behaviour, his majesty declaring, for his satisfaction, that it should not be interpreted a breach of good behaviour for him to reside in London, which was not consistent with the Oxford Act. After this release, he continued to live some time within the rules of the Bench; till, on the 28th of February, 1687, he removed to his house in the Charterhouse-yard; and again, as far as his health would permit, assisted Mr. Sylvester in his public labours.

'After his injurious confinement,' says his friend Sylvester, in the funeral sermon which he preached for Baxter, 'he settled in Charterhouse-yard, in Rutland-house, and bestowed his ministerial assistance gratis upon me. Thereupon he attended every Lord's Day in the morning, and every other Thursday morning at a weekly lecture. Thus were we yoked together in our ministerial work and trust, to our great mutual satisfaction; and because his respects to me, living and dying, were very great, I cannot but the more feel the loss. I had the benefit and pleasure of always free access to him, and instant conversation with him; and

by whom could I profit more than by himself? So ready
was he to communicate his thoughts to me, and so clearly
would he represent them, as that I may truly say, it was
greatly my own fault, if he left me not wiser than he found
me at all times.

'When, after about four years and a half he had continued
with me, he was then disabled from going forth any more
to his ministerial work; so that what he did, he performed
it all the residue of his life in his own hired house, where
he opened his doors morning and evening every day to all
that would come to join in family worship with him; to
whom he read the Holy Scriptures, from whence he
"preached the kingdom of God, and taught those things
which concern the Lord Jesus Christ, with all confidence,
no man forbidding him" (Acts 28:30, 31), even as one
greater than himself had done before him.

'But, alas! his growing distempers and infirmities took
him also from this, confining him first to his chamber, and
after to his bed. There, through pain and sickness his body
wasted; but his soul abode rational, strong in faith and hope,
arguing itself into, and preserving itself in that patience,
hope, and joy, through grace, which gave him great support,
and kept out doubts and fears concerning his eternal
welfare.'

He still laboured with his pen. Even on the very borders
of eternity he was desirous to improve the moments of his
time. 'He continued to preach,' Dr. Bates observes, in his
funeral discourse for his friend, 'so long, notwithstanding
his wasted, languishing body, that the last time he almost
died in the pulpit. Not long after, he felt the approaches of
death, and was confined to his sick bed. Death reveals the
secrets of the heart; then words are spoken with most feeling

and least affectation. This excellent saint was the same in his life and death; his last hours were spent in preparing others and himself to appear before God. He said to his friends that visited him, "You come hither to learn to die; I am not the only person that must go this way. I can assure you, that your whole life, be it ever so long, is little enough to prepare for death. Have a care of this vain, deceitful world, and the lusts of the flesh; be sure you choose God for your portion, heaven for your home, God's glory for your end, his Word for your rule, and then you need never fear but we shall meet with comfort."

'Never was penitent sinner more humble, never was a sincere believer more calm and comfortable. He acknowledged himself to be the vilest dunghill worm (it was his usual expression) that ever went to heaven. He admired the Divine condescension to us, often saying, "Lord, what is man? what am I, vile worm, to the great God!" Many times he prayed, "God be merciful to me a sinner," and blessed God that this was left upon record in the gospel as an effectual prayer. He said, "God may justly condemn me for the best duty I ever did; all my hopes are from the free mercy of God in Christ," which he often prayed for.

'After a slumber, he waked, and said, "I shall rest from my labour." A minister, then present, said, "And your works will follow you." To whom he replied, "No works; I will leave out works, if God will grant me the other." When a friend was comforting him with the remembrance of the good many had received by his preachings and writings, he said, "I was but a pen in God's hands, and what praise is due to a pen?"

'His resigned submission to the will of God in his sharp

sickness was eminent. When extremity of pain constrained him earnestly to pray to God for his release by death, he would check himself: "It is not fit for me to prescribe – when Thou wilt, what Thou wilt, how Thou wilt."

'Being in great anguish, he said, "Oh! how unsearchable are His ways, and his paths past finding out! the reaches of his providence we cannot fathom!" And to his friends, "Do not think the worse of religion for what you see me suffer."

'Being often asked by his friends, how it was with his inward man, he replied, "I bless God I have a well-grounded assurance of my eternal happiness, and great peace and comfort within." But it was his trouble he could not triumphantly express it, by reason of his extreme pains. He said, "Flesh must perish, and we must feel the perishing of it;" and that though his judgment submitted, yet sense would still make him groan.

'Being asked by a person of quality, whether he had not great joy from his believing apprehensions of the invisible state, he replied, "What else, think you, Christianity serves for?" He said, the consideration of the Deity, in his glory and greatness, was too high for our thought; but the consideration of the Son of God in our nature, and of the saints in heaven, whom he knew and loved, did much sweeten and familiarize heaven to him. The description of it, in Hebrews 12:22-24, was most comfortable to him; "that he was going to the innumerable company of angels, and to the general assembly and church of the firstborn, whose names are written in heaven; and to God the Judge of all, and to the spirits of just men made perfect, and to Jesus the Mediator of the new covenant, and to the blood of sprinkling that speaketh better things than the blood of Abel." That scripture, he said, deserved a thousand thousand thoughts. Oh, how comfortable is that promise, "Eye, hath not seen, nor ear heard, neither have entered into the heart of man, the things which God hath prepared for them that love him"! At another time, he said, that he found great comfort and sweetness in repeating the words of the Lord's Prayer, and was sorry some good people were prejudiced against the use of it, for there were all necessary petitions for soul and body contained in it.

'At other times, he gave excellent counsel to young ministers that visited him; earnestly prayed to God to bless their labours, and make them very successful in converting many souls to Christ; expressed great joy in the hopes that God would do a great deal of good by them; and that they were of moderate, peaceful spirits.

'He often prayed that God would be merciful to this miserable, distracted world, and that he would preserve his church and interest in it. He advised his friends to beware of self-conceit, as a sin that was likely to ruin this nation; and said, "I have written a book against it, which I am afraid has done little good." Being asked, whether he had altered his mind in controversial points, he said, "Those that please may know my mind in my writings;" and that what he had done was not for his own reputation, but for the glory of God.

'I went to him, with a very worthy friend, Mr. Mather, of New England, the day before he died; and speaking some comforting words to him, he replied, "I have pain; there is no arguing against sense; but I have peace, I have peace." I told him, "You are now approaching to your long-desired home." He answered, "I believe, I believe." He said to Mr. Mather, "I bless God that you have accomplished your business; the Lord prolong your life." He expressed his great willingness to die; and during his sickness, when the question was asked, "How he did?" his reply was, "Almost well." His joy was most remarkable, when, in his own apprehensions, death was nearest; and his spiritual joy was at length consummated in eternal joy.'

'As to himself, even to the last,' says Mr. Sylvester, 'I never could perceive his peace and heavenly hopes assaulted or disturbed. I have often heard him greatly lament himself, in that he felt no greater liveliness in what appeared so great and clear to him, and so very much desired by him. As to the influence thereof upon his spirit, in order to the sensible refreshments of it, he clearly saw what ground he had to rejoice in God; he doubted not of his right to heaven. He told me, he knew it would be well with him when he was gone. He wondered to hear others speak of their so sensible passionately strong desires to die, and of their transports of spirit when sensible of their approaching death; when, as he himself thought he knew as much as they, and had as rational satisfaction as they could have, that his soul was safe, and yet could never feel their sensible consolations. And when I asked, whether much of this was not to be resolved into bodily constitution, he did indeed tell me that he thought it might be so. But I have often thought, that God wisely made him herein, as in many other things, conformable to his great Master, Jesus Christ, whose joys we find commonly the fruit of deep and close thought. Christ argued himself into his own comforts. Which thing is evident from scriptures not a few: take, for a taste, Psalm 16:8-11; Hebrews 12:2.

'The testimony of his conscience was ever his rejoicing; like that in 2 Corinthians 1:12. He ever kept that tender; and gave such diligence to run his race, fulfil his ministry,

and so to make his calling and election firm and clear, as
that I cannot but conclude an entrance was ministered
abundantly to his departed spirit into the everlasting
kingdom of his God and Saviour, and that it will be more
abundant to his raised person when the Lord appears. The
heavenly state cost him severe and daily thoughts, and
solemn contemplations; for he set some time apart every
day for that weighty work. He knew that neither grace nor
duty could be duly actuated without pertinent and serious
meditation. What can be done without thought? And, as he
was a scribe instructed to the kingdom of heaven, so he
both could and did draw forth out of his treasures things
new and old, to his own satisfaction and advantage, as
well as to the benefit of others.

'He had frequently, before his death, owned to me his
continuance in the same sentiments that he had discovered
to the world before his polemical discourses, especially
about justification, and the covenants of works and grace,
etc. And being asked, at my request, whether he had changed
his former thoughts about those things, his answer was:
That he had told the world sufficiently his judgment
concerning them by words and writing, and thither he
referred men. And then, lifting up his eyes to heaven, he
uttered these words: "Lord, pity, pity, pity the ignorance of
this poor city."

'On Monday, the day before, about five in the evening,
death sent his harbinger to summon him away. A great
trembling and coldness awakened nature, and extorted
strong cries from him for pity and redress from heaven;
which cries and agony continued for some time, till at length
he ceased those cries, and so lay in an observant, patient
expectation of his change. And being once asked by a grave

matron, and his faithful friend and constant attendant upon him in his weakness, worthy and faithful Mrs. Bushel, his housekeeper, whether he knew her or no, requesting some signification of it if he did, he softly cried, "Death, death!" And now he felt the benefit of his former preparations for such a trying time as this. And, indeed, the last words that he spake to me, being informed that I was come to see him, were these: "O, I thank him, I thank him;" and, turning his eyes to me, he said, "The Lord teach you to die."

'On Tuesday morning, about four of the clock, December 8th, 1691, he expired; though he expected and desired his dissolution to have been on the Lord's Day before, which, with joy, to me he called a high day, because of his desired change expected then by him.'

A report was quickly spread abroad after his death that he was exercised on his dying bed with doubts respecting the truths of religion, and his own personal safety, which report by Sylvester thus indignantly refutes:

'What will degenerate man stick at? We know nothing here that could, in the least, minister to such a report as this. I, that was with him all along, have ever heard him triumphanting in his heavenly expectation, and ever speaking like one that could never have thought it worth a man's while to be, were it not for the great interest and ends of godliness. He told me that he doubted not but that it would be best for him when he had left this life and was translated to the heavenly regions.

'He owned what he had written, with reference to the things of God, to the very last. He advised those that came near him carefully to mind their souls' concerns. The shortness of time, the instancy [immediate importance] of eternity, the worth of souls, the greatness of God, the riches of the grace of Christ, the excellency and import of an heavenly mind and life, and the great usefulness of the Word and means of grace pursuant to eternal purposes, ever lay pressingly upon his own heart, and extorted from him very useful directions and encouragements to all that came near to him, even to the last; insomuch that if a polemical or casuistical point, or any speculation in philosophy or divinity, had been but offered to him for his resolution, after the clearest and briefest representation of his mind, which the proposer's satisfaction called for, he presently and most delightfully fell into conversation about what related to our Christian hope and work.'

Baxter was buried in Christ-church, where the ashes of his wife and her mother had been deposited. His funeral was attended by a great number of persons of different ranks, especially of ministers, conformists as well as nonconformists, who were eager to testify their respect for one of whom it might have been said with equal truth, as of John Knox, the intrepid reformer of the north, 'There lies the man who never feared the face of man.'

In his last will, made two years before his death, he says, 'I, Richard Baxter, of London, clerk, an unworthy servant of Jesus Christ, drawing to the end of this transitory life, having, through God's great mercy, the free use of my understanding, do make this my last will and testament, revoking all other wills formerly made by me.

'My spirit I commit, with trust and hope of the heavenly felicity, into the hands of Jesus, my glorified Redeemer and Intercessor; and, by his mediation, into the hands of God, my reconciled Father, the infinite, eternal Spirit, Light, Life, and Love, most great and wise and good, the God of nature, grace, and glory; of whom, and through whom, and to whom, are all things; my absolute Owner, Ruler, Benefactor, whose I am, and whom I, though imperfectly, serve, seek, and trust; to whom be glory for ever, Amen.

'To Him I render the most humble thanks, that he hath filled up my life with abundant mercy, and pardoned my sins by the merits of Christ, and vouchsafed, by his Spirit, to renew me and seal me as his own; and to moderate and bless to me my long sufferings in the flesh, and at last to sweeten them by his own interest, and comforting approbation.' He bequeathed his books to 'poor scholars', and the residue of his property to the poor.

8

Character of Richard Baxter

Having proceeded to the grave, and committed his 'remains' to their long and final resting-place, it will be desirable to present the views which were formed of his character by his friends.

'His person,' Sylvester states, 'was tall and slender, and stooped much; his countenance composed and grave, somewhat inclining to smile. He had a piercing eye, a very articulate speech, and his deportment rather plain than complimental. He had a great command over his thoughts. He had that happy faculty, so as to answer the character that was given of him by a learned man dissenting from him, after discourse with him; which was, that "he could say what he would, and he could prove what he said." '

Extracts from funeral sermon by Dr. Bates
Dr. Bates has drawn a full-length portrait of the character of his venerable friend in his funeral sermon, from which some extracts will now be given.

'He had not the advantage of academical education; but, by the Divine blessing upon his rare dexterity and diligence, his sacred knowledge was in that degree of eminence, as few in the university ever arrive to.'

'Conversion is the excellent work of Divine grace; the efficacy of the means is from the supreme Mover. But God usually makes those ministers successful in that blessed

work, whose principal design and delight is to glorify him
in the saving of souls. This was the reigning affection in
his heart; and he was extraordinarily qualified to obtain
his end.

'His prayers were an effusion of the most lively, melting
expressions, and his intimate ardent affections to God: from
the abundance of his heart his lips spake. His soul took
wing for heaven, and wrapped up the souls of others with
him. Never did I see or hear a holy minister address himself
to God with more reverence and humility, with respect to
his glorious greatness; never with more zeal and fervency
correspondent to the infinite moment of his requests; nor
with more filial affiance in the Divine mercy.'

Dr. Bates says, 'In his sermons there was a rare union
of arguments and motives to convince the mind and gain
the heart. All the foundations of reason and persuasion were
open to his discerning eye. There was no resisting the force
of his discourses, without denying reason and Divine
revelation. He had a marvellous felicity and copiousness
in speaking. There was a noble negligence in his style; for
his great mind could not stoop to the affected eloquence of
words: he despised flashy oratory, but his expressions were
clear and powerful; so convincing the understanding, so
entering into the soul, so engaging the affections, that those
were as deaf as adders who were not charmed by so wise
a charmer. He was animated by the Holy Spirit, and
breathed celestial fire to inspire heat and life into dead
sinners, and to melt the obdurate in their frozen tombs.
Methinks I still hear him speak those powerful words: "A
wretch that is condemned to die to-morrow cannot forget
it: and yet poor sinners, that continually are uncertain to
live an hour, and certain speedily to see the majesty of the

Lord, to their inconceivable joy or terror, as sure as they now live on earth, can forget these things, for which they have their memory; and which, one would think, should drown the matters of this world as the report of a cannon does a whisper or as the sun obscures the poorest glow-worm. O wonderful stupidity of an unrenewed soul! O wonderful folly and distractedness of the ungodly! That ever man can forget, I say again, that they forget, eternal joy, eternal woe, and the eternal God, and the place of their eternal, unchangeable abodes, when they stand even at the door; and there is but that thin veil of flesh between them and that amazing sight, that eternal gulf, and they are daily dying and stepping in." '

To this may be added a quotation from a sermon preached before the judges at the assizes: 'Honourable, worshipful, and all well-beloved, it is a weighty employment that occasioneth your meeting here today. The estates and lives of men are in your hands. But it is another kind of judgment which you are all hastening towards: when judges and juries, the accusers and accused, must all appear upon equal terms, for the final decision of a far greater cause. The case that is then and there to be determined is not whether you shall have lands or not lands, life or no life, in our natural sense; but whether you shall have heaven or hell, salvation or damnation, an endless life of glory with God, the Redeemer, and the true angels of heaven, or an endless life of torment with devils and ungodly men. As sure as you now sit on those seats, you shall shortly all appear before the Judge of all the world, and there receive an irreversible sentence to an unchangeable state of happiness or misery. This is the great business that should presently call up your most serious thoughts, and set all the powers of your souls on work for the most effectual preparation; that, if you are men, you may acquit yourselves like men, for the preventing of that dreadful doom which unprepared souls must there expect. The greatest of your secular affairs are but dreams and toys to this. Were you, at every assize, to determine causes of no lower value than the crowns and kingdoms of the monarchs of the earth, it were but as children's games to this. If any man of you believe not this, he is worse than the devil that tempteth him to unbelief; and let him know that unbelief is no prevention, nor will put off the day, or hinder his appearance, but ascertain his condemnation at that appearance.

'He that knows the law and the fact, may know, before your assize, what will become of every prisoner, if the proceedings be all just, as in our case they will certainly be. Christ will judge according to his laws; know, therefore, whom the law condemneth or justifieth, and you may know whom Christ will condemn or justify. And seeing all this is so, doth it not concern us all to make a speedy trial of ourselves in preparation to this final trial? I shall, for your own sakes, therefore, take the boldness, as the officer of Christ, to summon you to appear before yourselves, and keep an assize this day in your own souls, and answer at the bar of conscience to what shall be charged upon you. Fear not the trial; for it is not conclusive, final, or a peremptory irreversible sentence that must not pass. Yet slight it not; for it is a necessary preparative to that which is final and irreversible.'

After describing the vanities of the world, he bursts forth, 'What! shall we prefer a mole-hill before a kingdom? A shadow before the substance? An hour before eternity? Nothing before all things? Vanity and vexation before felicty? The cross of Christ hath set up such a sun as quite darkeneth the light of worldly glory. Though earth were something, if there were no better to be had, it is nothing when heaven standeth by.'

Dr. Bates further remarks, 'Besides, his wonderful diligence in catechising the particular families under his charge was exceeding useful to plant religion in them. Personal instruction, and application of Divine truths, has an excellent advantage and efficacy to insinuate and infuse religion into the minds and hearts of men, and, by the conversion of parents and masters, to reform whole families that are under their immediate direction and government. His unwearied industry to do good to his flock was answered by correspondent love and thankfulness. He was an angel in their esteem. He would often speak with great complacence of their dear affections; and, a little before his death, said, "he believed they were more expressive of kindness to him than the Christian converts were to the apostle Paul, by what appears in his writings."

'His books, for their number and variety of matter in them, make a library. They contain a treasure of controversial, casuistical, positive, and practical divinity. Of them I shall relate the words of one whose exact judgment, joined with his moderation, will give a great value to his testimony; they are of the very reverend Dr. Wilkins, afterwards Bishop of Chester. He said that Mr. Baxter had "cultivated every subject he handled"; and "if he had lived in the primitive times, he had been one of the fathers of the church." I shall add what he said with admiration of him another time: "That it was enough for one age to produce such a person as Mr. Baxter." Indeed, he had such an amplitude in his thoughts, such a vivacity of

imagination, and such solidity and depth of judgment, as
rarely meet together. His inquiring mind was freed from
the servile dejection and bondage of an implicit faith. He
adhered to the Scriptures as the rule of faith, and searched
whether the doctrines received and taught were consonant
to it. This is the duty of every Christian, according to his
capacity, especially of ministers, and the necessary means
to open the mind for Divine knowledge, and for the
advancement of the truth.

'His books of practical divinity have been effectual for
more numerous conversions of sinners to God than any
printed in our time; and, while the church remains on earth,
will be of continual efficacy to recover lost souls. There
is a vigorous pulse in them that keeps the reader awake
and attentive. His book of the *Saints' Everlasting Rest*
was written by him when languishing in the suspense of
life and death, but has the signatures [marks] of his holy
and vigorous mind. To allure our desires, he unveils the
sanctuary above and discovers the glory and joys of the
blessed in the Divine presence, by a light so strong and
lively that all the glittering vanities of this world vanish in
that comparison and a sincere believer will despise them
as one of mature age does the toys and baubles of children.
To excite our fear he removes the screen and makes the
everlasting fire of hell so visible, and represents the
tormenting passions of the damned in those dreadful colours,
that, if duly considered, would check and control the
unbridled licentious appetites of the most sensual
wretches.'

Baxter's practical writings alone occupy four ponderous
folio, or twenty-two octavo volumes. If a complete
collection of his controversial and practical writings were

made, they would occupy fully sixty volumes of the same size. 'His industry was almost incredible in his studies. He had a sensitive nature, desirous of ease, as others have, and faint faculties, yet such was the continual application of himself to his great work, as if the labour of one day had supplied strength for another, and the willingness of the spirit had supported the weakness of the flesh.' His painful and incessant afflictions would have prevented an ordinary man from attempting anything; but he persevered, with unwearied industry, to the close of his days. His life was occupied, too, in active labours. In camps and at court, in his parish and in prison, at home and abroad, his efforts were unremitting, and often successful.

Some idea of his sufferings may be formed from the summary of his diseases given by his late biographer.

'His constitution was naturally sound, but he was always very thin and weak, and early affected with nervous debility. At fourteen years of age he was seized with the small-pox, and soon after, by improper exposure to the cold, he was affected with a violent catarrh and cough. This continued for about two years, and was followed by spitting of blood, and other phthisical [lung disease] symptoms. He became, from that time, the sport of medical treatment and experiment. One physician prescribed one mode of cure, and another a different one; till, from first to last, he had the advice of no less than thirty-six professors of the healing art. By their orders he took drugs without number, till, from experiencing how little they could do for him, he forsook them entirely, except some particular symptom urged him to seek present relief. He was diseased literally from head to foot; his stomach flatulent and acidulous; violent rheumatic headaches; prodigious

bleeding at the nose; his blood so thin and acrid that it
oozed out from the points of his fingers, and kept them
often raw and bloody; his legs swelled and dropsical, etc.
His physicians called it hypochondria; he himself
considered it *præmatura senectus*, premature old age; so
that at twenty he had the symptoms, in addition to disease,
of fourscore! To be more particular would be disagreeable;
and to detail the innumerable remedies to which he was
directed, or which he employed himself, would add little
to the stock of medical knowledge. He was certainly one
of the most diseased and afflicted men that ever reached
the full ordinary limits of human life. How, in such
circumstances, he was capable of the exertions he almost
incessantly made, appears not a little mysterious. His
behaviour under them is a poignant reproof to many, who
either sink entirely under common afflictions, or give way
to indolence and trifling. For the acerbity [sourness] of his
temper we are now prepared with an ample apology. That
he should have been occasionally fretful, and impatient of
contradiction, is not surprising, considering the state of the
earthen vessel in which his noble and active spirit was
deposited. No man was more sensible of his obliquities of
disposition than himself; and no man, perhaps, ever did
more to maintain the ascendency of Christian principle over
the strength and waywardness of passion.'

The conviction that his time would be short urged him
to prosecute his labours with unwearied assiduity. Love to
immortal souls, too, exerted its powerful influence. This
'love to the souls of men,' says Dr. Bates, 'was the peculiar
character of his spirit. In this he imitated and honoured our
Saviour, who prayed, died, and lives for the salvation of
souls. All his natural and supernatural endowments were

subservient to that blessed end. It was his meat and drink, the life and joy of his life, to do good to souls.'

Disinterestedness formed no unimportant feature of his character, and was strikingly marked in his refusal of ecclesiastical preferment; his self-denying engagements respecting his stipend at Kidderminster; his gratuitous labours; abundant alms-giving; and in the wide distribution of his works among the poor and destitute. So long as he had a bare maintenance, he was content. He rejoiced in being able to benefit others by his property or his labours.

Fidelity to his Divine Master and to His cause was conspicuous in all his engagements. He tendered his advice or administered his reproofs with equal faithfulness, whether in court or camp; to the king or to Cromwell; before Parliament or his parishioners; in his conversation or his correspondence. He could not suffer sin upon his neighbour; and whatever he conceived would be for the benefit of the parties concerned, that he faithfully, and without compromise, administered. In his preaching he 'shunned not to declare the whole counsel of God,' and, in consequence, was free from the blood of all men.

Dr. Bates remarks: 'He that was so solicitous for the salvation of others was not negligent of his own; but, as regular love requires, his first care was to prepare himself for heaven. In him the virtues of the comptemplative and active life were eminently united. His time was spent in communion with God, and in charity to men. He lived above the sensible world, and in solitude and silence conversed with God. The frequent and serious meditation of eternal things was the powerful means to make his heart holy and heavenly, and from thence his conversation. His life was a practical sermon, a drawing example. There was an air of humility and sanctity in his mortified countenance; and his deportment was becoming a stranger upon earth, and a citizen of heaven.'

The following passage from his interesting, important work entitled *The Divine Life* may be considered as a portrait of his own spiritual character: 'To walk with God is a word so high that I should have feared the guilt of arrogance in using it, if I had not found it in the Holy Scriptures. It is a word that importeth so high and holy actions that the naming of it striketh my heart with reverence, as if I had heard the voice to Moses, "Put off thy shoes from off thy feet, for the place whereon thou standest is holy ground." Methinks, he that shall say to me, Come see a man that walks with God, doth call me to see one that is next unto an angel or glorified soul. It is a far more reverend object in mine eye than ten thousand lords or princes, considered only in their fleshly glory. It is a wiser action for people to run and crowd together to see a man that walks with God than to see the pompous train of princes, their entertainments, or their triumph. Oh, happy man that walks with God, though neglected and contemned by all about him! What blessed sights doth he daily see! What ravishing tidings, what pleasant melody doth he daily hear! What delectable food doth he daily taste! He seeth that in a glass, and darkly, which they behold with open face! He seeth the glorious majesty of his Creator, the eternal King, and Cause of causes, the Composer, Upholder, Preserver, and Governor of all worlds! He beholdeth the wonderful methods of his providence; and what he cannot reach to see, he admireth, and waiteth for the time when that also shall be open to his view! He seeth, by faith, the world of spirits, the hosts that attend the throne of God; their perfect righteousness, their full devotedness to God; their ardent love, their flaming zeal, their ready and cheerful obedience, their dignity and shining glory, in which the lowest of them exceed that which the disciples saw on Moses and Elias, when they appeared on the holy mount and talked with Christ! He hears by faith the heavenly concert, the high and harmonious songs of praise, the joyful triumphs of crowned saints, the sweet commemorations of the things that were done and suffered on earth, with the praises of Him that redeemed them by His blood, and made them kings and priests unto God. Herein he hath sometimes a sweet foretaste of the everlasting pleasures which, though it be but little, as Jonathan's honey on the end of his rod, or as the clusters of grapes which were brought from Canaan into the wilderness, yet is more excellent than all the delights of sinners.'

His character may be summed up in the words of Mr. Orme: 'Among his comtemporaries there were men of equal talents, of more amiable dispositions, and of greater learning. But there was no man in whom there appears to have been so little of earth, and so much of heaven; so small a portion of the alloy of humanity, and so large a portion of all that is celestial. He felt scarcely any of the attractions of this world, and felt and manifested the most powerful affinity for the world to come.'

9

Baxter's Personal Review

Some few years before his death, Baxter took a minute and extensive survey of his own character, and committed it to paper. From this paper the following extracts are taken:

'Because it is soul-experiments which those that urge me to this kind of writing do expect that I should especially communicate to others, and I have said little of God's dealing with my soul since the time of my younger years, I shall only give the reader so much satisfaction, as to acquaint him truly what change God hath made upon my mind and heart since those unriper times, and wherein I now differ in judgment and disposition from myself. And, for any more particular account of heart-occurrences, and God's operations on me, I think it somewhat unsavoury to recite them; seeing God's dealings are much the same with all his servants in the main, and the points wherein he varieth are usually so small, that I think not such fit to be repeated. Nor have I anything extraordinary to glory in, which is not common to the rest of my brethren, who have the same Spirit, and are servants of the same Lord. And the true reason why I do adventure so far upon the censure of the world, as to tell them wherein the case is altered with me, is that I may take off young, inexperienced Christians from being over-confident in their first apprehensions, or overvaluing their first degrees of grace, or too much applauding and following unfurnished, inexperienced men, but may somewhat be directed what mind and course of life to prefer, by the judgment of one that hath tried both before them.

'The temper of my mind hath somewhat altered with the temper of my body. When I was young, I was more vigorous, affectionate, and fervent in preaching, conference and prayer than ordinarily I can be now; my style was more extemporary and lax, but by the advantage of affection, and a very familiar moving voice and utterance, my preaching then did more affect the auditory than many of the last years before I gave over preaching; but yet what I delivered was much more raw, and had more passages that would not bear the trial of accurate judgments, and my discourses had both less substance and less judgment than of late.

'My understanding was then quicker, and could more easily manage anything that was newly presented to it upon a sudden; but it is since better furnished, and acquainted with the ways of truth and error, and with a multitude of particular mistakes of the world, which then I was the more in danger of, because I had only the faculty of knowing them, but did not actually know them. I was then like a man of a quick understanding, that was to travel a way which he never went before, or to cast up an account which he never laboured in before, or to play on an instrument of music which he never saw before; and I am now like one of somewhat a slower understanding, by that *præmatura senectus* [premature old age], which weakness and excessive bleedings brought me to, who is travelling a way which he hath often gone, and is casting up an account which he hath often cast up, and hath ready at hand, and that is playing on an instrument which he hath often played on: so that I can very confidently say, that my judgement is much sounder and firmer now than it was then; and I can now judge of the effects, as well as of the actings of my own understanding; and, when I peruse the writings which I wrote in my younger years, I can find the footsteps of my unfurnished mind, and of my emptiness and insufficiency: so that the man that followed my judgment then was more likely to have been misled by me than he who should follow it now.

'And yet, that I may not say worse than it deserveth of my former measure of understanding, I shall truly tell you what change I find now, in the perusal of my own writings. Those points, which then I thoroughly studied, my judgment is the same of now, as it was then; and therefore, in the substance of my religion, and in those controversies which I then searched into, with some extraordinary diligence, I find not my mind disposed to a change. But in divers points that I studied slightly, and by the halves, and in many things which I took upon trust from others, I have found since that my apprehensions were either erroneous, or very lame.

'And I must say farther, that what I last mentioned on the bye, is one of the most notable changes of my mind. In my youth I was quickly past my fundamentals, and was running up into a multitude of controversies, and greatly delighted with metaphysical and scholastic writings, though, I must needs say, my preaching was still on the necessary points. But, the older I grew, the smaller stress I laid upon these controversies and curiosities, (though still my intellect abhorreth confusion,) as finding far greater uncertainties in them, than I at first discerned, and finding less usefulness comparatively, even where there is the greatest certainty. And now it is the fundamental doctrines of the catechism which I most highly value, and daily think of, and find most useful to myself and others. The Creed, the Lord's Prayer and the Ten Commandments do find me now the most acceptable and plentiful matter for all my meditations. They are to me as my daily bread and drink. And, as I can speak and write of them over and over again, so I had rather read or hear of them than of any of the school niceties which once so much pleased me. And thus I observed it was with old Archbishop Usher, and with many other men; and I conjecture that this effect also is mixed of good and bad, according to its causes.

'The bad cause may, perhaps, be some natural infirmity and decay. And as trees, in the spring, shoot up into branches, leaves, and blossoms, but, in the autumn, the life draws down into the root, so possibly my nature, conscious of its infirmity and decay, may find itself insufficient for numerous particles, and to rise up for the attempting of difficult things, and so my mind may retire to the root of Christian principles; and also I have often been afraid, lest ill-rooting at first, and many temptations afterwards, have made it more necessary for me than many others to retire to the root, and secure my fundamentals. But, upon much observation, I am afraid lest most others are in no better a case; and that, at the first, they take it for a granted thing that Christ is the Saviour of the world, and that the soul is immortal, and that there is a heaven and a hell, etc. while they are studying abundance of scholastic superstructures, and at last will find cause to study more soundly their religion itself, as well as I have done.

'The better causes are these:

'1. I value all things according to their use and ends; and I find, in the daily practice and experience of my soul, that the knowledge of God and Christ, and the Holy Spirit, and the truth of Scripture, and the life to come, and of a holy life, is of more use to me than all the most curious speculations.

'2. I know that every man must grow, as trees do, downwards and upwards both at once, and that the roots increase as the bulk and branches do.

'3. Being nearer death, and another world, I am the more regardful of those things which my everlasting life or death depend on.

'4. Having most to do with ignorant, miserable people, I am commanded, by my charity and reason, to treat with them of that which their salvation lieth on, and not to dispute with them of formalities and niceties, when the question is presently to be determined, whether they shall dwell for ever in heaven or in hell.

'In a word, my meditations must be most upon the matters of my practice and my interest; and as the love of God, and the seeking of everlasting life, is the matter of my practice and my interest, so must it be of my meditation. That is the best doctrine and study, which maketh man better and tendeth to make them happy. I abhor the folly of those unlearned persons who revile or despise learning because they know not what it is; and I take not any part of true learning to be useless. And yet my soul approveth of the resolution of holy Paul who determined to know nothing among his hearers – that is, comparatively to value and make ostentation of no other wisdom – but the knowledge of a crucified Christ. To know God in Christ is eternal. As the stock of the tree affordeth timber to build houses and cities, when the small, though higher multifarious branches are but to make a crow's nest or a blaze; so the knowledge of God and of Jesus Christ, of heaven and holiness, doth build up the soul to endless blessedness and affordeth it solid peace and comfort, when a multitude of school niceties serve but for vain janglings, and hurtful diversions and contentions. I would persuade any reader to study and live upon the essential doctrines of Christianity and godliness. And, that he may know that my testimony is somewhat regardable, I presume to say that in this I as much gainsay my natural inclination to subtilty and accurateness in knowing, as he is like to do by his, if he obey my counsel. And I think, if he lived among infidels and enemies of Christ, he would find that to make good the doctrine of faith and of life eternal were not only his noblest and most useful study, but also that which would require the height of all his parts, and the utmost of his diligence, to manage it skilfully to the satisfaction of himself and others.

'I add, therefore, that this is another thing which I am changed in; that whereas, in my younger days, I never was tempted to doubt of the truth of Scripture or Christianity, but all my doubts and fears were exercised at home, about my own sincerity and interest in Christ, and this was it which I called unbelief. Since then, my sorest assaults have been on the other side; and such they were that, had I been void of internal experience, and the adhesion of love, and the special help of God, and had not discerned more reason for my religion than I did when I was younger, I had certainly apostatised to infidelity, though, for atheism or ungodliness, my reason seeth no stronger arguments than may be brought to prove that there is no earth, or air, or sun. I am now, therefore, much more apprehensive than heretofore of the necessity of well grounding men in their religion, and especially of the witness of the indwelling Spirit; for I more sensibly perceive that the Spirit is the great witness of Christ and Christianity to the world.

'And though the folly of fanatics tempted me long to overlook the strength of this testimony of the Spirit, while they placed it in a certain internal assertion, or enthusiastic inspiration, yet now I see that the Holy Ghost, in another manner, is the witness of Christ and his Agent in the world. The Spirit in the prophets was his first witness, and the Spirit by miracles was the second; and the Spirit by renovation, sanctification, illumination, and consolation, assimilating the soul to Christ and heaven, is the continued witness to all true believers. And if any man have not the Spirit of Christ, the same is none of his (Rom. 8:9); even as the rational soul in the child is the inherent witness, or evidence, that he is the child of rational parents. And, therefore ungodly persons have a great disadvantage in their resisting temptations to unbelief, and it is no wonder if Christ be a stumbling-block to the Jews, and to the Gentiles foolishness. There is many a one that hideth his temptations to infidelity, because he thinketh it a shame to open them, and because it may generate doubts in others; but, I fear, the imperfection of most men's care of their salvation, and of their diligence and resolution in a holy life, doth come from the imperfection of their belief of Christianity and the life to come. For my part, I must profess, that when my belief of things eternal, and of the Scripture, is most clear and firm, all goeth accordingly in my soul, and all temptations to sinful compliances, worldliness, or flesh-pleasing, do signify worse to me than an invitation to the stocks or Bedlam; and no petition seemeth more necessary to me than, "Lord, increase our faith: I believe, help thou my unbelief."

'In my younger years, my trouble for sin was most about

my actual failings in thought, word or action, except hardness of heart, of which more anon; but now I am much more troubled for inward defects, and omission or want of the vital duties or graces in the soul. My daily trouble is so much for my ignorance of God, and weakness of belief, and want of greater love to God, and strangeness to him, and to the life to come, and for want of a greater willingness to die, and longing to be with God in heaven, as that I take not some immoralities, though very great, to be in themselves such great and odious sins, if they could be found as separate from these. Had I all the riches of the world, how gladly should I give them for a fuller knowledge, belief, and love of God and everlasting glory! These wants are the greatest burdens of my life, which often make my life itself a burden. And I cannot find any hope of reaching so high in these, while I am in the flesh, as I once hoped before this time to have attained; which maketh me the wearier of this sinful world, which is honoured with so little of the knowledge of God.

'Heretofore I placed much of my religion in tenderness of heart, and grieving for sin, and penitential tears; and less of it in the love of God, and studying his love and goodness, and in his joyful praises, than I now do. Then I was little sensible of the greatness and excellency of love and praise, though I coldly spake the same words in its commendation as I now do. And now I am less troubled for want of grief and tears, though I more value humility, and refuse not needful humiliation; but my conscience now looketh at love and delight in God, and praising him, as the top of all religious duties, for which it is that I value and use the rest.

'My judgment is much more for frequent and serious

meditation on the heavenly blessedness, than it was heretofore in my younger days. I then thought that a sermon on the attributes of God, and the joys of heaven, were not the most excellent; and was wont to say, "Everybody knoweth this, that God is great and good, and that heaven is a blessed place; I had rather hear how I may attain it." And nothing pleased me so well as the doctrine of regeneration, and the marks of sincerity, because these subjects were suitable to me in that state; but now I had rather read, hear or meditate on God and heaven than on any other subject; for I perceive that it is the object that altereth and elevateth the mind which will be such as that is which it most frequently feedeth on; and that it is not only useful to our comfort to be much in heaven in our believing thoughts, but that it must animate all our other duties and fortify us against every temptation and sin; and that the love of the end is the poise, or spring, which setteth every wheel agoing, and must put us on to all the means; and that a man is no more a Christian indeed than he is heavenly.

'I was once wont to meditate most on my own heart, and to dwell all at home, and look little higher. I was still poring either on my sins or wants, or examining my sincerity; but now, though I am greatly convinced of the need of heart-acquaintance and employment, yet I see more need of a higher work; and that I should look often upon Christ and God and heaven than upon my own heart. At home I can find distempers to trouble me, and some evidences of my peace; but it is above that I must find matter of delight and joy, and love and peace itself. Therefore I would have one thought at home upon myself and sins, and many thoughts above upon the high and amiable and beatifying [blessed] objects.

'Heretofore I knew much less than now, and yet was not half so much acquainted with my ignorance. I had a great delight in the daily new discoveries which I made, and of the light which shined in upon me, like a man that cometh into a country where he never was before; but I little knew, either how imperfectly I understood those very points, whose discovery so much delighted me, nor how much might be said against them, nor how many things I was yet a stranger to; but now I find far greater darkness upon all things, and perceive how very little it is that we know in comparison of that which we are ignorant of; and I have far meaner thoughts of my own understanding though I must needs know that it is better furnished than it was then.

'Accordingly, I had then a far higher opinion of learned persons and books than I have now; for what I wanted myself, I thought every reverend divine had attained, and was familiarly acquainted with. And what books I understood not, by reason of the strangeness of the terms or matter, I the more admired, and thought that others understood their worth. But now, experience hath constrained me, against my will, to know that reverend learned men are imperfect and know but little as well as I, especially those who think themselves the wisest; and the better I am acquainted with them, the more I perceive that we are all yet in the dark. And the more I am acquainted with holy men, that are all for heaven and pretend not much to subtilties, the more I value and honour them. And when I have studied hard to understand some abstruse admired book as *De Scientiâ Dei*, *De Providentiâ circa malum*, *De Decretis*, *De Prædeterminatione*, *De Libertate Creaturæ* etc., I have but attained the knowledge of human imperfection and to see that the author is but a man as well as I.

'And at first I took more upon my author's credit than now I can do. And when an author was highly commended to me by others, or pleased me in some part, I was ready to entertain the whole; whereas now I take and leave in the same author and dissent in some things from him that I like best, as well as from others.

'At first the style of authors took as much with me as the argument, and made the arguments seem more forcible; but now I judge not of truth at all by any such ornaments or accidents, but by its naked evidence.

'I now see more good and more evil in all men than heretofore I did. I see that good men are not so good as I once thought they were, but have more imperfections; and that nearer approach, and fuller trial, doth make the best appear more weak and faulty than their admirers at a distance think. And I find that few are so bad as either their malicious enemies or censorious separating professors do imagine. In some, indeed, I find that human nature is corrupted into a greater likeness to devils than I once thought any on earth had been; but even in the wicked, usually there is more for grace to make advantage of, and more to testify for God and holiness, than I once believed there had been.

'I less admire gifts of utterance, and bare profession of religion, than I once did; and have much more charity for many who, by the want of gifts, do make an obscurer profession than they. I once thought that almost all that could pray movingly and fluently, and talk well of religion, had been saints. But experience hath opened to me what odious crimes may consist with high profession; and I have met with divers obscure persons, not noted for any extraordinary profession, or forwardness in religion, but only to live a quiet blameless life, whom I have after found to have long lived, as far as I could discern, a truly godly and sanctified life; only their prayers and duties were, by accident, kept secret from other men's observation. Yet he that, upon this pretence, would confound the godly and the ungodly may as well go about to lay heaven and hell together.

'I am not so narrow in my special love as heretofore. Being less censorious, and talking more than I did for saints, it must needs follow that I love more as saints than I did before.

'I am much more sensible how prone many young professors are to spiritual pride and self-conceitedness, and unruliness and division (and so to prove the grief of their teachers) and firebrands in the church; and how much of a minister's work lieth in preventing this, and humbling and confirming such young, inexperienced professors and keeping them in order in their progress in religion.

'Yet am I more sensible of the sin and mischief of using men cruelly in matters of religion, and of pretending men's good, and the order of the church, for acts of inhumanity and uncharitableness. Such know not their own infirmity, nor yet the nature of pastoral government, which ought to be paternal, and by love; nor do they know the way to win a soul, nor to maintain the church's peace.

'I am more deeply afflicted for the disagreements of Christians than I was when I was a younger Christian. Except the case of the infidel world, nothing is so sad and grievous to my thoughts as the case of the divided churches; and, therefore, I am more deeply sensible of the sinfulness of those prelates and pastors of the churches who are the principal cause of these divisions. Oh, how many millions of souls are kept by them in ignorance and ungodliness, and deluded by faction as if it were true religion! How is the conversion of infidels hindered by them, and Christ and religion heinously dishonoured! The contentions between the Greek church and the Roman, the Papists and the Protestants, the Lutherans and the Calvinists, have woefully hindered the kingdom of Christ.

'I am farther than ever I was from expecting great matters of unity, splendour or prosperity to the church on earth, or that saints should dream of a kingdom of this world, or flatter themselves with the hopes of a golden age, or reigning over the ungodly, till there be a new heaven and a new earth, wherein dwelleth righteousness. And, on the contrary, I am more apprehensive that sufferings must be the church's most ordinary lot, and Christians indeed must be self-denying cross-bearers, even where there are none but formal, nominal Christians to be the cross-makers. And though, ordinarily, God would have vicissitudes of summer and winter, day and night, that the church may grow extensively in the summer of prosperity, and intensively and rootedly in the winter of adversity; yet, usually, their night is longer than their day, and that day itself hath its storms and tempests.

'I do not lay so great a stress upon the external modes and forms of worship as many young professors do. I have suspected myself, as perhaps the reader may do, that this is from a cooling and declining from my former zeal, though the truth is, I never much complied with men of that mind; but I find that judgment and charity are the causes of it, as far as I am able to discover. I cannot be so narrow in my principles of church communion as many are, that are so much for a liturgy or so much against it; so much for ceremonies or so much against them, that they can hold communion with no church which is not of their mind and way. If I were among the Greeks, the Lutherans, the Independents, yea, the Anabaptists, that own no heresy, nor set themselves against charity and peace, I would hold, sometimes, occasional communion with them as Christians, if they will give me leave, without forcing me to any sinful subscription or action; though my most usual communion should be with that society which I thought most agreeable to the Word of God, if I were free to choose. I cannot be of their opinion that think God will not accept him that prayeth by the common prayer-book, and that such forms are a self-invented worship which God rejecteth: nor yet can I be of their mind that say the like of extemporary prayers.

'I am much less regardful of the approbation of man and set much lighter by contempt or applause, than I did long ago. I am often suspicious that this is not only from the increase of self-denial and humility, but partly by my being glutted and surfeited with human applause; and all worldly things appear most vain and unsatisfactory when we have tried them most. But though I feel that this hath some hand in the effect, yet, as far as I can perceive, the knowledge of man's nothingness, and God's transcendent greatness (with whom it is that I have most to do), and the sense of brevity of human things, and the nearness of eternity, are the principal causes of this effect, which some have imputed to self-conceitedness and moroseness.

'I am more and more pleased with a solitary life; and though, in a way of self-denial, I could submit to the most public life for the service of God when he requireth it, and would not be unprofitable that I might be private; yet, I must confess, it is much more pleasing to myself to be retired from the world, and to have very little to do with men, and to converse with God and conscience and good books.

'Though I was never much tempted to the sin of covetousness, yet my fear of dying was wont to tell me that I was not sufficiently loosened from the world. But I find that it is comparatively very easy to me to be loose from this world, but hard to live by faith above. To despise earth is easy to me; but not so easy to be acquainted and conversant in heaven. I have nothing in this world which I could not easily let go; but to get satisfying apprehensions of the other world is the great and grievous difficulty.

'I am much more apprehensive than long ago of the odiousness and danger of the sin of pride: scarce any sin appeareth more odious to me. Having daily more acquaintance with the lamentable naughtiness and frailty of man, and of the mischiefs of that sin, and, especially, in matters spiritual and ecclesiastical, I think, so far as any man is proud, he is kin to the devil, and utterly a stranger to God and to himself. It is a wonder that it should be a possible sin to men that still carry about with them, in soul and body, such humbling matter of remedy as we all do.

'I more than ever lament the unhappiness of the nobility, gentry and great ones of the world who live in such temptation to sensuality, curiosity and wasting of their time about a multitude of little things; and whose lives are too often the transcript of the sins of Sodom – pride, fulness of bread, and abundance of idleness, and want of compassion to the poor. And I more value the life of the poor labouring man, but especially of him that hath neither poverty nor riches.

'I am much more sensible than heretofore of the breadth and length and depth of the radical, universal and odious sin of selfishness, and therefore have written so much against it: and of the excellency and necessity of self-denial, and of a public mind, and of loving our neighbour as ourselves.

'I am more and more sensible that most controversies have more need of right stating than of debating; and, if my skill be increased in anything, it is in that in narrowing controversies by explication, and separating the real from the verbal, and proving to many contenders that they differ less than they think they do.

'I am more solicitous than I have been about my duty to God, and less solicitous about his dealings with me, as being assured that he will do all things well; and as acknowledging the goodness of all the declarations of his holiness, even in the punishment of man, and as knowing that there is no rest but in the will and goodness of God.

'Though my works were never such as could be any temptation to me to dream of obliging God by proper merit, in commutative justice, yet one of the most ready, constant, undoubted evidences of my uprightness and interest in his covenant is the consciousness of my living as devoted to him. And I the more easily believe the pardon of my failings, through my Redeemer, while I know that I serve no other Master, and that I know no other end or trade or business; but that I am employed in His work, and make it the business of my life, with my longing desires after perfection in the knowledge and belief and love of God, and in a holy and heavenly mind and life, are the two standing, constant, discernible evidences which most put me out of doubt of my sincerity. And I find that constant action and duty is it that keepeth the first always in sight; and constant wants and weaknesses and coming short of my desires do make those desires still the more troublesome, and so the more easily still perceived.

'Though my habitual judgment and resolution and scope
of life be still the same, yet I find a great mutability as to
actual apprehensions and degrees of grace; and, consequently, find that so mutable a thing as the mind of man
would never keep itself, if God were not its keeper. When
I have been seriously musing upon the reasons of
Christianity, with the concurrent evidences methodically
placed in their just advantages before my eyes, I am so
clear in my belief of the Christian verities that Satan hath
little room for a temptation. But, sometimes, when he hath
on a sudden set some temptations before me, when the
foresaid evidences have been out of the way or less upon
my thoughts, he hath by such surprises amazed me and
weakened my faith in the present act. So also as to the love
of God and trusting in him, sometimes, when the motives
are clearly apprehended, the duty is more easy and
delightful. And at other times I am merely passive and dull,
if not guilty of actual despondency and distrust.

'Thus much of the alterations of my soul since my
younger years I thought best to give the reader, instead of
all those experiences and actual motions and affections
which I suppose him rather to have expected an account
of. And having transcribed thus much of a life which God
hath read, and conscience hath read, and must further read,
I humbly lament it and beg pardon of it as sinful, and too
unequal and unprofitable. And I warn the reader to amend
that in his own which he findeth to have been amiss in
mine; confessing, also, that much hath been amiss which I
have not here particularly mentioned, and that I have not
lived according to the abundant mercies of the Lord. But
what I have recorded hath been especially to perform my
vows, and declare his praise to all generations, who hath

filled up my days with his invaluable favours, and bound me to bless his name for ever.

'But having mentioned the changes which I think were for the better, I must add that, as I confessed many of my sins before, so, since I have been guilty of many, which, because materially they seemed small, have had the less resistance, and yet, on the review, do trouble me more than if they had been greater, done in ignorance. It can be no small sin which is committed against knowledge and conscience and deliberation, whatever excuse it have. To have sinned whilst I preached and wrote against sin, and had such abundant and great obligations from God, and made so many promises against it, doth lay me very low; not so much in fear of hell, as in great displeasure against myself, and such self-abhorrence as would cause revenge upon myself were it not forbidden. When God forgiveth me, I cannot forgive myself; especially for any rash words or deeds by which I have seemed injurious and less tender and kind than I should have been to my near and dear relations, whose love abundantly obliged me. When such are dead, though we never differed in point of interest or any great matter, every sour or cross provoking word which I gave them maketh me almost irreconcilable to myself, and tells me how repentance brought some of old to pray to the dead whom they had wronged, in the hurry of their passion, to forgive them.

'And, though I before told the change of my judgment against provoking writings, I have had more will than skill to avoid such. I must mention it, by way of penitent confession, that I am too much inclined to such words, in controversial writings, as are too keen and apt to provoke the person whom I write against. Sometimes I suspect that

age soureth my spirits, and sometimes I am apt to think that
it is long thinking and speaking of such things that maketh
me weary, and less patient with others that understand them
not. And sometimes I am ready to think that it is out of
hatred of the flattering humour, which now prevaileth so in
the world, that few persons are able to bear the truth: and I
am sure that I cannot only bear myself such language as I
use to others, but that I expect it. I think all these are partly
causes: but I am sure the principal cause is a long custom
of studying how to speak and write in the keenest manner
to the common, ignorant and ungodly people, without which
keenness to them, no sermon nor book does much good;
which hath so habituated me to it that I am still falling into
the same with others; forgetting that many ministers and
professors of strictness do desire the greatest sharpness to
the vulgar, and to their adversaries, and the greatest lenity
and smoothness and comfort, if not honour, to themselves.
And I have a strong natural inclination to speak of every
subject just as it is, and to call a spade a spade and to suit
the word to the occasion, so as that the thing spoken of may
be most fully known by the words, which, methinks, is part
of our speaking truly.

'But I unfeignedly confess that it is faulty, because
imprudent; for that is not a good means which doth harm,
because it is not fitted to the end; and because, whilst the
readers think me angry, though I feel no passion at such
times in myself, it is scandalous and a hindrance to the
usefulness of what I write. And especially because, though
I feel no anger, yet, which is worse, I know that there is
some want of honour and love, or tenderness to others, or
else I should not be apt to use such words as open their
weakness and offend them. And therefore I repent of it and

wish all over-sharp passages were expunged from my writings, and desire forgiveness of God and man. And yet I must say that I am often afraid of the contrary extreme, lest when I speak against great and dangerous errors and sins, though of persons otherwise honest, I should encourage men to them by speaking too easily of them, as Eli did to his sons, and lest I should so favour the person as may befriend the sin and wrong the church.

'And, therefore, I am less for a disputing way than ever, believing that it tempteth men to bend their wits to defend their errors and oppose the truth, and hindereth usually their information. And the servant of the Lord must not strive, but be gentle to all men, etc. Therefore I am most in judgment for a learning or a teaching way of converse. In all companies, I will be glad either to hear those speak that can teach me, or to be heard of those that have need to learn.

'And that which I named before on the bye is grown one of my great diseases. I have lost much of that zeal which I had to propagate any truths to others, save the mere fundamentals. When I perceive people or ministers, which is too common, to think they know what indeed they do not, and to dispute those things which they never thoroughly studied, or expect I should debate the case with them, as if an hour's talk would serve instead of an acute understanding and seven years' study, I have no zeal to make them of my opinion, but an impatience of continuing discourse with them on such subjects, and am apt to be silent, or to turn to something else; which, though there be some reason for it, I feel cometh from a want of zeal for the truth, and from an impatient temper of mind. I am ready to think that people should quickly understand all in a few words; and, if they cannot, lazily to despair of them and leave them to themselves. And I the more know that it is sinful in me, because it is partly so in other things, even about the faults of my servants, or other inferiors; if three or four times' warning do no good on them, I am much tempted to despair of them, and turn them away and leave them to themselves.

'I mention all these distempers, that my faults may be a warning to others to take heed, as they call on myself for repentance and watchfulness. O Lord, for the merits and sacrifice and intercession of Christ, be merciful to me a sinner and forgive my known and unknown sins.'

INDEX

Other volumes in the Historymakers Series

Henry Havelock by John Pollock
ISBN 185792 245X   B format 304 pp

Pastor Hsi by Geraldine Taylor
ISBN 185792 1593   B format 240304

Martin Luther by Thomas Lindsay
ISBN 185792 2611   B format 240 pp

Robert Murray McCheyne by Alexander Smellie
ISBN 185792 1844   B format 256 pp

Moody Without Sankey by John Pollock
ISBN 185792 1674   B format 320 pp

George Muller by Roger Steer
ISBN 185792 3405   B format 256 pp

John Owen by Andrew Thomson
ISBN 185792 2670   B format 192 pp

Charles Simeon by Handley Moule
ISBN 185792 3103   B format 240 pp

Hudson (Taylor) and Maria by John Pollock
ISBN 185792 2239   B format 208 pp